Achieve professional results
by improving your approach to conflict

Do you know how to keep your cool in the midst of misunderstandings, arguments and insults?

In Confidence in Conflict for Everyday Life you'll learn to:

- Alter your reality by accepting and anticipating conflict
- Control your approach by correctly reading the situation and responding to others
- Reframe your outlook by delivering respect (even when it's hard)
- Appear confident and capable
- Master first impressions

See for yourself how the professional strategies of Verbal Defense & Influence can be used within the everyday setting of your personal life.

These strategies are taught through the Vistelar Group, which has trained some of the world's most suc ssan USA. Other clients include the secu ica, and police agencies across the countr and Kalamazoo, MI.

D1166732

www.ConfidenceinConflict.com

Hear from our readers...

"This small and powerful book lays out an excellent set of directions for navigating your way through the day ... I recommend for young and old alike - never too young, never too old to learn a few simple skills for minimizing conflict."

— *Roy Aiken*

"Conflict is inevitable and confidence in communicating while in conflict has never been my strong skill set. Your book is full of helpful everyday tactics."

— *Katherine Isgren*

"I wish I had it when my daughter was still in her teens. I could have used a handbook on how better to treat my family members, particularly when my buttons were being pushed. I would have been better off responding using the techniques outlined in this book and not reacting."

— *John Fallon, English professor, Rhodes State College, Lima, OH*

"The best thing I enjoyed about reading the book was the clear explaining of the simple sequence to follow during any given situation and identifying the responsibilities people have by providing those options and understanding others and how respond to them. I will make this a mandatory reading for several classes I teach to help students improve their future performance."

— *Dave Young, Arma Training*

"Ms. Mangold has done the research, talked to the experts, lived the lessons she is teaching. Her book takes you though the steps and teaches you the skills needed to deal with virtually any situation in a calm and controlled manner. I highly recommend this book for anyone who wants or needs to learn to deal with conflict (and who among us does not?) from the grocery store to the bank to the workplace to driving in the car.

— *Tae Kwon Do Master Paul Callahan*

"At last, we have a step-by-step template for how to manage conflict written by and for the average person. Based on decades of public safety experience, we now have a travel guide for conflict management directed toward personal interactions rather than professional ones. This is a book based on day-to-day, real-life verbal conflict that every one of us must maneuver through each day.

"While most of this conflict is verbal in nature, it can escalate to the point of physical danger, even assault. This training, prepares you to survive the full spectrum of human conflict. Kathy Mangold in her many roles of mother, low-level conflict resolution specialist, and professional writer shows us the way through the minefield of "normal" personal and social interactions. This an easy read that with further review & study will prepare readers for survival in the increasing complex and conflict-ridden world that we live."

— *Gary T. Klugiewicz, Director, Verbal Defense & Influence*

Confidence In Conflict For Everyday Life

Proven strategies for conflict resolution and communicating under pressure

Kathy Mangold
Edited by Colin J. Hahn, Ph.D.

Truths Publishing
Milwaukee, WI

www.ConfidenceInConflict.com

For bulk-purchase pricing, please contact:

Vistelar Group
1845 N. Farwell Ave., Suite 210
Milwaukee, Wis., 53202
Phone: 877-690-8230
Fax: 866-406-2374
Email: info@vistelar.com
Web: www.vistelar.com

Mangold, Kathy
   Confidence In Conflict For Everyday Life / by Kathy Mangold
Edited by Colin J. Hahn, Ph.D.
   ISBN 13: 978-0-9792734-0-7
   ISBN 10: 0-9792734-0-4

LCCN:
   2014939434

BSAC Subject Headings:
   FAM013000   FAMILY & RELATIONSHIPS / Conflict Resolution
   SEL040000 SELF-HELP / Communication & Social Skills

Published by Truths Publishing, Milwaukee, WI
Printed in the United States of America

Build your skills

Resources and opportunities inspire further learning

As you read through Confidence in Conflict for Everyday Life, you'll see that this book draws heavily upon stories of everyday conflict, told by people around the country who use Verbal Defense & Influence skills to communicate.

SIGN UP FOR FREE: You can hear them discuss their struggles and achievements in the types of situations that many of us encounter every day. By visiting www.ConfidenceinConflict.com/PeaceStories, you'll see how people from all professions and walks of life use our strategies to resolve conflict and communicate under pressure.

DIG EVEN DEEPER: This book is only the beginning. These concepts are explained and reinforced in Confidence in Conflict for Everyday Life: Online Course. Enhance your learning through instructional videos, real-life examples and activities. Visit www.ConfidenceinConflict.com/OnlineCourse.

"When you commit to managing yourself in the midst of conflict, you are less susceptible to conflict."
— Confidence in Conflict for Everyday Life

Table of Contents

1: Alter your reality:
How to accept and anticipate conflict — 23
Fairy tales, Hollywood and Disney hijack our expectations for relationships. The fact is, conflict is present in our everyday lives. In this chapter, you will discover why anticipating and managing your aggravators is the first crucial step in holding your emotions steady.

2: Master your approach:
How to read the situation and respond to others — 33
Fools rush in. Tactical thinkers, on the other hand, get command of the facts and take decisive action.

3: Reframe your outlook:
How to show respect, even when it's hard — 41
Your outlook drives your actions. And if your goal is to be effective in all of your encounters, your mission should be to treat people right.

4: It's Showtime!
How to appear confident and capable — 51
What's Showtime? It's the best way to describe the mental and physical process of putting on your game face.

10: Moving ahead:

COMMUNICATING UNDER PRESSURE

FIVE MAXIMS

BE ALERT & DECISIVE

RESPOND, DON'T REACT

"SHOWTIME" MINDSET

UNIVERSAL GREETING

BEYOND ACTIVE LISTENING

REDIRECTIONS

PERSUASION SEQUENCE

Bystander Mobilization

When Words Alone Fail

REVIEW • REPORT

WWW.VISTELAR.COM

Preface

The little things in our lives do matter.

Understanding this is the key point in resolving conflict in everyday life, within the relationships that matter most.

Having the ability to recognize smoke before a fire erupts heightens your awareness, making you more alert to potential hazards. Having the skills that let you stay functional and focused in the midst of pressure keeps you effective, no matter what.

We'll start by diving into the concept of conflict, and then ultimately discover how to handle ourselves when conflict is present.

Too often, conflict is portrayed in black-and-white terms. There is a dragon and a hero. There must be a threat and the hero must triumph. There are winners and there are losers.

Oh, but that's not how conflict looks in my life, and I'll bet it doesn't look that way in yours, either. The problems that cause me the most grief don't occur with dragons: they happen among my family, friends and co-workers.

We're not enemies; we are simply in conflict.

And that's an important point: unless we know how to come back together and smooth out the minor disruptions, we find ourselves saying and doing things that push us even further apart.

Most of us tend to react in one of two ways. Some of us will react by shutting down, retreating to our corner and avoiding the problem altogether. Others will puff up, get defensive and barge right into the fray.

Neither of these approaches will resolve a thing.

Reacting badly, even to small mishaps and misunderstandings, sets a course for a negative chain of events. It doesn't take much for interactions to sour or for relationships to crumble into bits.

A recently divorced friend of mine summed up how the divide between her and her partner pushed them apart until eventually, their relationship ceased to function:

"We drifted apart, and couldn't find our way back," she said about their breakup.

It wasn't a big, monstrous dragon that struck the fatal blow; it was the thousand little gremlins that wouldn't stop biting.

My purpose in writing this book is to help you build a framework for communicating in everyday conflict that is based upon professional conflict resolution strategies.

In this book you will learn about Verbal Defense & Influence, a methodology developed and taught by the Vistelar Group. You'll discover a set of strategies that keeps children bully-proof at school and professionals safe and effective on the job.

But, most of all, you will expand your personal capacity for identifying and addressing conflict within your own relationships:

- Can you create and maintain a peaceable environment, even when others are resistant?
- Can you defuse a situation that is escalating into drama?
- Can you effectively communicate and resolve conflict in the heat of the moment?

My grandma used to playfully tell my brother and I to "fight nice" whenever we started to bicker, and it always sounded so funny to me. Now that I teach Verbal Defense & Influence, I think that Grandma's weird advice was on the right track. Grandma didn't tell us to quiet down or stop arguing. She knew that the key to resolving the situation was managing conflict respectfully.

She'd be so proud that I've found a set of skills to keep conflict from getting the best of me. She'd be even more proud to learn that these skills inspire confidence in people from all walks of life, today and every day.

Introduction:

Getting unstuck

"I just need to know what to do in the 30 seconds after a blowout."
— Jenny K., elementary school principal

It was a surprise to me when Jenny, a seasoned elementary school principal, revealed to me her shortcoming: a momentary indecisiveness at the point of crisis. She was (and still is) one of the most competent, pragmatic and self-assured school administrators around.

Jenny does all the right things. Her building is well ordered, her staff is upbeat, and her students are respectful, all of which reflect her careful management. When a crisis does occur, she has reporting policies and follow-up procedures in place.

But there's volatility nonetheless. Pressure-filled moments can be anticipated, but they cannot be known in advance. One moment it will take the shape of an angry parent raging into her office, or a fender bender in the parking lot. Another moment, it will be the crying student who must be soothed.

What forms your response

As a responsible leader, Jenny might feel the need to rush headfirst into the storm, intervene and prevent problems (anything from minor irritations to full-blown emergencies) from getting worse.

The moment of impact is the point of crystallization, when Jenny's skills, mindset, beliefs and instincts mesh to form her response.

This is the point at which Jenny might wish for a magic wand.

What she actually needs is a consistent method for dealing with conflict, something that is effective in all situations. Her best case scenario would be to have strategies that can be applied at home as well as at work.

That's an important point here. Having the skills to keep you cool at work should transition into your personal life, and enrich the relationships that matter most.

A consistent approach

The moment someone is the least bit obstructive, it can knock us off our game. For some of us, a bad attitude and some verbal resistance will shatter our calm.

To make matters worse, we're often not the ones with the problem—the other person is. The client is unreasonable, the patient is irritating or the student is impossible.

And what if this unreasonable person happens to be your mother-in-law? You need solid help.

Yeah they're the problem all right, but the answer has to come from you. You aren't the problem, but you bring the solution.

To explain this idea, our trainers use this quote in their classes. It comes from the North Dakota Highway Patrol:

"We treat people like ladies and gentlemen not necessarily because they are, but because we are."

When someone challenges us, we need the skills to act as the ladies and gentlemen that we are. This is when we need to know how to respond in an effective manner during stressful interactions instead of impulsively reacting.

In this book I'll show you how to use the Verbal Defense & Influence methodology to develop a consistent approach for remaining effective, even in the thick of conflict. All of the strategies you will learn are based on utilizing the singular motivator that influences us all (no matter who we are).

We all want to be shown dignity and treated with respect, right?

The key to unlocking resistance is to turn dignity and respect into deliverables.

You see, when I treat another person with respect I am projecting empathy, which enables me to persuade, motivate and inspire an obstructive person. I can listen. I can keep my own emotions in check. I can stay focused on resolving the issue at hand. Then once the dust settles, I can review my actions and improve the future.

Time for a tune-up

The onus is on us to maintain ourselves. And that's an ongoing task. If we don't respond correctly to all those bumps in the road, they manifest themselves as dissatisfaction, embitterment, burnout and compassion fatigue.

These things can throw off our groove to the point that we confront the decision: shoulder on or leave.

A few years ago during a Verbal Defense & Influence training program for baseball umpires, I made a surprising observation. The audience consisted of two groups: grizzled old veterans, and newbies barely able to shave. There were only a few 30-year-olds to be found.

Why?

The ones who learned strong coping mechanisms at some point in their umpire careers stuck it out, while others, somewhere in midlife, dropped off along the way. Then there were the young ones, who had so much to learn.

As the enforcer of the rules, the role an umpire plays can be so confrontational that they are forced to develop coping mechanisms to deal with the verbal abuse, or they get off the field.

I looked around at the young faces in the room. Could their love of baseball withstand the relentless pressure they would encounter game after game?

Can you stay in the game?

The prospect of facing a season's worth of "toughening up"—or two or six seasons—isn't exactly ideal. But that's how we learn coping skills.

We typically transition from inexperienced to functional to proficient by learning things the hard way, in both our jobs and our relationships.

If you're lucky you might have a mentor who can rub off a little wisdom. Some professions embed this relationship into their training (such as a doctor's residency) while other professions leave the experience-gaining process to time—or worse yet—to chance.

But no one has the time for that. We can't wait for experience to show up on our doorstep, like the delivery guy who comes late with cold and soggy pizza. Here are the hazards of waiting around for experience to come a-knocking:

1. Effective communication under pressure is a learnable skill, but it isn't taught anywhere.
2. Communication skills develop slowly over time, but the world isn't going to stop long enough for us to reach a state of competency.
3. Even if you're a natural communicator, it's tough to pass along that gift to others.
4. We're always being watched—anyone witnessing us at work, home or the grocery store has the capability of pulling out their phones and recording us in the midst of conflict, thereby capturing the good, the bad and almost certainly the ugly.

The longer we wait, the more we risk losing personal satisfaction and time. Without a doubt our personal effectiveness hinges on our ability to focus, stay in control and have a plan.

Fortunately there's a better way than trial by fire to learn the principles of communicating under pressure.

About us

In a very short amount of time, the Vistelar Group has gone from a basement startup company to a global training program experiencing tremendous growth—the need is great for a training program that aims to shift perspectives and impart skills.

The skills are based on time-tested communications strategies that have been vetted through studies and tested in high-intensity communications settings for more than 30 years.

It's no overstatement to say the professionals who participate in Verbal Defense & Influence training encounter every type of conflict imaginable. In any given class we see a mixture of beat cops, prison wardens, city workers and security staff from casinos, malls, hospitals and campuses.

For them, pushback, resistance and conflict are part of the day's work. And they are savvy enough to know what will work at the point of impact and what will not.

It doesn't take them long to buy in and see that Verbal Defense & Influence strategies can change the way they do business. But they're really hooked when, just a few moments later, they understand something even more important:

You can change your life, too. When you commit to managing yourself in the midst of conflict, you are less susceptible to conflict.

We see it all the time in the review sheets that students turn in at the end of class. People appreciate how this makes them more efficient in the conflict that happens at work. But what we hear over and over again is how they've learned to become more balanced and capable of responding to pressure at home.

Think about that for a minute. These people oversee society's most violent criminals. And here they are, thanking us: partly for how this stuff works with bad guys, but mostly because it works in managing conflict in their personal lives.

A little bit of background

We owe our methodology to a long line of contributors and practitioners who have developed and refined the principles that have crystallized in the form taught today.

The verbal tactics for managing conflict, often referred to as "verbal self-defense," were the subject of dozens of books during the 1980s.

Suzette Haden Elgin wrote one of the first books: The Gentle Art of Verbal Self-Defense, first published in 1980. She went on to publish twelve more books on this subject, including How to Disagree Without Being Disagreeable. Other authors included George Thompson (Verbal Judo: The Gentle Art of Persuasion), Sam Horn (Tongue Fu: How To Deflect, Disarm and Diffuse Any Verbal Conflict), Lillian Glass (The Complete Idiot's Guide to Verbal Self-Defense) and Daniel Scott (Verbal Self Defense for the Workplace).

Between the early 80s and the next three decades, verbal self-defense training was widely adopted by police departments. Many trainers within the fields of law enforcement, corrections and mental health pioneered programming in Wisconsin, most notably Vistelar Director Gary T. Klugiewicz and his mentors such as Daniel Vega and Jane Dresser.

Dr. George Thompson, whose Verbal Judo principles were a great influence, was a member of the Vistelar Group until his death in 2011. For a number of years he consulted with me on writing projects and developing learning materials.

It is worth noting that these tactics continue to be refined and expanded as they are field-tested and applied in our greatly changing world. It is fitting, therefore, to offer sincere thanks to those who contribute feedback, share their experiences and keep our offerings relevant and dynamic.

In the last year we've helped communities become stronger. We recently spent some time at the U.S. headquarters for Nissan USA, training their top management, and taught children in schools around the country how to bully-proof themselves and build confidence.

"The Verbal Defense & Influence methodology is an essential skill," said Kevin M. Gilmartin, Ph.D., author of Emotional Survival. "It completes the balanced package of necessary survival skills for those required to have a continuum of expertise in resolving confrontational situations."

As one of the public faces for the company (through our public relations, conferences and other outreach), I've helped shape the vision for Vistelar. In the weekly newsletter I write, I share tips for workplace effectiveness and personal growth.

You know what? The stories that receive the most feedback are the ones that touch people on a personal level, and I know why. We all have family and friends that hold the ability to lift us up and bring us down.

More joy, less stress. So stay with me—that's where we're headed.

Just follow the directions

Why do you need a framework for communicating under pressure? At presentations I use the analogy of a recipe card because we're all familiar with this structure: a foolproof set of instructions for replicating success.

While some cooks can throw together two handfuls of flour, a few eggs, some sugar and apples and make a passable concoction, it's hard to make it again with reasonable consistency, let alone share the instructions with others.

But when I pull out my apple cake recipe, I am confident it is going to turn out as well as it always does.

That structure makes it possible to replicate success, and teach it to others.

The same thing happens when I have a practiced response to unpredictable or volatile situations. Having a framework gives me the insight to respond pragmatically and consistently.

That structure makes it possible to replicate success, and teach it to others.

A skill for the ages

We're all at a different place when it comes to our ability to manage conflict:

- Some of us react instinctively—and end up doing/saying things we regret.
- Some of us get knocked off balance as soon as an interaction starts to sour, and we lose our confidence immediately.
- Some of us exhibit moments of brilliance amid conflict, when we can stand up for ourselves and persuade others.

Other times we fail miserably. But we never look back to assess what we did wrong—or right.

- Some of us have a knack for managing conflict, but because it comes "naturally," we can't explain what we're doing. That means it's extremely difficult to pass along this skill to others.

Regardless of our level of ability, we are all trapped in a pattern of reacting the same way over and over again.

The ability to communicate and function in the midst of stress is a skill for life. Consider the poster hanging in the corner of the orchestra room at my son's middle school, encouraging students to practice their skills on their instruments. It reads:

"Amateurs practice until they get it right. Professionals practice until they can't get it wrong."

It's time to stop hoping that conflict strategies will magically develop over time. It's time to apply this skill-focused mindset to the presence we display in times of stress.

It's time to get unstuck.

Chapter 1

Alter your reality:

How to accept and anticipate conflict

Overview: *Fairy tales, Hollywood and Disney hijack our expectations for relationships. The fact is, conflict is present in our everyday lives. In this chapter, you will discover why anticipating and managing your aggravators is the first crucial step in holding your emotions steady.*

Consider, for a moment, the language sometimes used to describe "perfect" relationships:

- Friends are best friends forever.
- True love is a match with your soulmate.
- Romance culminates in happily ever after.

The whole idea of conflict is inconsistent with that image of perfection.

Could that be why so many of us hide from conflict or pretend it doesn't exist?

Respectful resolution is hard to find

Hollywood, Disney and happily-ever-after have done a great disservice to the complexity of our lives.

Not only do we delude ourselves into believing conflict shouldn't exist, we rarely see examples of how to handle it.

There are scarce examples in our world that portray the amicable resolution of disagreement.

Here's a little challenge for you: look around in today's world and see if you can find a working model in which a plurality of viewpoints exists and functions in a respectful way.

Does healthy debate take place within politics? Hmm. It seems vicious and unbalanced to me.

What about conflict resolution on TV? The drama involved in relationships portrayed on TV doesn't reflect my life (thank goodness) and neither do the celebrities who make the cover of People magazine.

Conflict is either nonexistent (thanks, Disney) or blown out of proportion (thanks, Jersey Shore).

You can hardly be surprised that many of us, in our everyday lives, avoid conflict at every turn. Should conflict start to rev up, we don't possess an instruction manual for turning off the machine.

Quite simply, once conflict is present we don't know how to make it stop.

Conflict happens. The best defense is preparedness, which you might not have possessed until now.

If you've ever said the words …

- *How could you say that to me?*
- *Where did that come from? I thought we were friends.*
- *Why didn't you tell me? I deserve to know.*
- *What were you thinking? I can't believe you were so careless.*

… then this chapter is for you.

Conflict is inevitable

Conflict is a fact of life. But it's not something we prepare ourselves for, much less tell our children—at least I didn't. Until it was too late.

Best friends disagree. Couples argue. Co-workers have opposing viewpoints. We understand this on an intellectual level, but it can feel like a sucker-punch to the gut when it happens and we're not prepared.

I remember the first time my daughter Maria came home in tears because someone at school called her a name. It smacked her from out of the blue. She'd have been more resilient if I'd known to prepare her for that inevitability—no one gets through life insult-free. But I never took the time to prepare her for that, and being caught unaware was as raw as a slap in the face.

I wish I had sat my Maria down, before that first heartbreaking insult. I would have told her that she'd enter into conflict, even with her very best friends. I would have prepared her for the possibility.

Instead, she came home from second grade, emotional and raw, because she wasn't expecting that she and a BFF—best friend forever—could fall out of alignment, especially at an age when they're so desperately trying to fit in.

It was a scary possibility for her, that dissension of any type could lead to a major fallout.

But fortunately for Maria, the odds for resolution improve when we possess the skills to anticipate and handle discord.

LESSON 1 : Think when, not if

Confidence in conflict exists when you approach conflict from the perspective of when, not if.

One word will set your approach miles apart.

Vistelar Advisor Bob "Coach" Lindsey has developed the concept of "when-then thinking" to describe a better way for approaching conflict.

Having this operating philosophy lets me acknowledge the probability of conflict, and protects me against the potential for disruption.

Such a mindset paves the way toward managing my response. Now I can focus upon resolving situations, instead of letting them escalate out of control.

If I raise my daughter, for example, with the expectation that she and her classmates would have an occasional disagreement, she wouldn't conduct her interactions under the constant fear that discord with a friend would result in total collapse of their relationship.

Even as adults, we will fall out of harmony with our spouse. Our child will push our buttons. We will get smacked in the head with an insult we never expected.

Instead of letting it knock us off balance we can build resiliency—but first we need to acknowledge that it can happen, right?

How will this end?

If you're hoping that this book will hold some secret to eliminating conflict from your life, I'm really sorry. That's impossible.

Think back to my daughter, Maria, who felt her world shatter over her first minor brush with conflict. To this day she still needs gentle reminders that conflict will happen again and again. The potential is always there in the encounters that we find ourselves in.

There is going to be disagreement among those with whom we willingly enter into relationship (think spouses, lovers or friends).

Then consider the list of people we are compelled to interact with. That list is even longer: clients, patients, students, customers, rude salesclerks and perhaps current, ex- and step-relatives.

With anyone you encounter, your loyalty may be questioned, and so might your competency. The things that set you apart—appearance, preferences, values and passions—can be a source of strife.

The problem won't go away, but your response can change for the better. We all know people who are appear to sail through their days and their lives, unscathed by conflict.

What is it that these people do so well? They know how to prepare themselves in case conflict happens and defuse before the rest of us even notice something might be amiss.

Here's a case in point: when we were developing our anti-bullying curriculum we spent a lot of time deliberating what to name it. Ultimately we chose Manage Bullying, a name I liked then, and I still like now.

Some people didn't like it though. Manage bullying? Don't we want to eradicate bullying? Crush it? Blow it out of the water?

Not possible.

Those names miss the point. Bullying has been around forever; it probably happened among cavemen. Aggressors have asserted their power in the past, and will probably attempt to continue forever in the future. But they only succeed when the conditions are ripe.

If you can manage yourself and the situation, you can manage bullying.

There's no magic bullet, but the power to change is there—and it's all yours.

The next step requires mastering your emotional reactions.

LESSON 2: Guarding against anger and emotion

An Emotion Guard is like an invisible shield to protect you from the things that bug you and make you angry or sad.

Having mental control over your feelings lets you prevent any type of emotional excess, including anger and rage, shutting down, withdrawing or crying.

You can't let your initial, emotional reaction override your reasoned and rational response. If you let your emotions take over, you'll look unprofessional at best, or a hot mess at worst.

Building up Emotion Guards is a skill that must be learned—it doesn't come easily or naturally.

Neurological research has shown that when we are in the midst of stress our bodies experience very real physical changes to our bodies:

- Our adrenalin flow speeds up.
- Our blood pressure increases.
- Our breathing becomes shallow.
- Our ears shut down (this condition is called auditory exclusion).
- Our visual focus narrows (this is known as tunnel vision).
- Our fine motor skills deteriorate.

These physical conditions send panic signals to our brain.

Having the ability to put a shield over our emotions and consciously recognize these physiological messages lets us get control and gain some power over this purely neurological fight-or-flight response.

This is how when-then thinking enters into play. Notice how a when-then mindset changes everything:

"I know it sets me off when someone gets in my face. I need a shield for those situations."

When you set up a reality-based framework—when something happens then I have a response—it's easy to visualize and set up a course of action.

Your first steps in building a solid foundation require that you remove yourself from the wishful netherworld of *"it won't happen to me..."*

LESSON 3: Own your triggers

Knowledge is power. This is especially true when we are talking about self-discovery.

If I asked you to write down a list of things that cause your stress level to skyrocket, the list would be long and ugly. But there's value in taking an inventory here.

If you were to list these triggers on paper, you might find that they fall into certain categories (e.g., comments about your appearance, age, speech patterns) Having these tidy little classifications provides a measure of comfort. It gives you the opportunity to anticipate the things that had previously seemed to be smacking you from your blind side.

Here's an analogy. Having the ability to classify a problem reminds me of when I'd take my sick toddlers to the doctor. I could tell my child was in pain but, until they were able to speak, I had no idea why.

Visiting the doctor, having some tests and coming away with a clear diagnosis always gave me peace of mind.

I might not have liked the fact that they were suffering from, say, strep throat. But it was a relief to know that my child's pain had particular attributes I could understand and address.

The same is true with the triggers that cause us emotional pain. Once the triggers are "diagnosed," we can control our response to them.

Now let's illustrate how this works by showing what happens to my friend Bill whenever he encounters the thing that triggers him most... donuts.

Bill meets Mr. Donut

"Hey, want a donut?"

It's never been a funny question for Bill Singleton, a Milwaukee police officer and one of the masterminds behind the city's STOP Program (Students Talking it Over with Police), a program based on Vistelar's teachings. It is designed to break down barriers, demystify the job of law enforcement officers and overcome stereotypes that inhibit police-youth relations.

It's amazing, Bill says, how often he hears that comment when he is on duty and in uniform. It remains as un-funny and derogatory now as it was the first time he heard it, but there's nothing he (or any other police officer) can do to make it stop.

The D-word is a trigger for Bill, because it consistently makes him crazy.

But, because Bill has learned to anticipate this trigger, he has the ability to maintain his composure, acknowledge the insult and move on.

"When I hear someone talking about cops and donuts I stop and think to myself, 'Hey, I'm talking to Mr. Donut,'" he said. "Giving this trigger a label lets me laugh at the situation and move on."

Here's what Bill has learned to do:

- He identified the trigger (he recognizes his weakness: that he's bothered by the comments about donuts)
- He has engaged in when-then thinking and set up an Emotion Guard (he accepts that such comments won't go away, so he's created a response)
- He has given the trigger a name (*"Here comes Mr. Donut!"*)
- He can laugh and move on.

Think about what consistently angers you. What if you could stop your emotions from setting you off?

Boy meets trigger

Now that Bill understands his trigger, he can respond in a way that keeps him in control. He understands he could be called this name at any time, and he devised a shield that lets him control his emotions.

Owning your triggers is like unlocking a source of power to accept the things that set you off, to come to terms with them, and to move on.

Now let's consider a famously inappropriate response. Remember the folk song Johnny Cash used to sing about the boy named Sue? As the song goes, "Some gal would giggle and I'd get red, some guy would laugh and I'd bust his head..."

Poor Sue. The social stigma of having a girl's name was an unbearable thorn that got re-stuck under his skin every time he heard it.

Until the final showdown with his father, Sue was consistently volatile to his trigger. How much better would his life have been if he could have, right from the start, owned up to his trigger and controlled it?

In the end Sue finally reconciles with his father. The trajectory of this story line resonates with anyone who struggles with their own personal issue: Person struggles with trigger. Person enters into conflict based on trigger. Person gains perspective on trigger and moves along with his life.

You can't get back the angry years when your trigger made you crazy. But you can use the Verbal Defense & Influence skills to move ahead.

Conflict and you: A new attitude

Conflict is everywhere. Therefore it's not realistic to dive under the desk at the first sign of conflict. Conflict will crawl right under and find you.

Thank goodness you are learning our proven way to deal with conflict head-on.

CHAPTER 1 CHALLENGE

Using what you've learned about approaching conflict and developing Emotion Guards, consider these questions. Turn to the Communicating Under Pressure chart (page 12) and to see how the concepts covered in Chapter One fit in.

1. Has conflict brought you down? Name three instances of conflict you have had in the past month.

2. You can become more proactive by changing the way you ready yourself for conflict. Consider how you can reframe a situation by thinking in terms of when, not if.

3. How do you react when your hot button is pushed? List the things that consistently trip your trigger.

4. If you can name it, you can own it and control it. Consider how that message applies to the triggers you listed in #3.

Chapter 2

Master your approach:

How to read the situation and respond to others

Overview: Fools rush in. Tactical thinkers, on the other hand, get command of the facts and take decisive action.

After reading Chapter 1, you should have a baseline acceptance of this fact:

Conflict can arise any day—irritations, slights, misunderstandings, snubs or worse.

You're no longer engaging in that wishful, if-then thinking: *If conflict takes place then I'll worry about it.*

You know that a proactive response involves the when: *When one of my triggers is tripped I'll have a planned response.*

There's such power in making the switch.

But the only way this will happen is if you are plugged in and alert to the signs. This chapter will focus on two important concepts: being able to read the situation and responding appropriately.

Knowing when to take action

Being capable of taking an accurate reading of a situation is the first critical step in assessing your course of action.

Sounds simple enough to me but I can recall in vivid detail the times that I've acted without command of all the facts, and botched up everything, at home, at work and, quite memorably, in front of the principal at my kids' elementary school.

Knowing when to take action also means understanding the point at which you are losing effectiveness and need to move from words into further action. Depending on the situation this can include following through on a consequence or disengaging and getting help.

We'll get into this more in later chapters. For now, establishing your ability to be aware of situations and others around you is a good place to start.

LESSON 4: Adopt tactical thinking

The word "tactical" has been relegated to the hard-hitting world of physical conflict and I'm on a mission to bring it back to the rest of us.

I began my love affair with the word "tactical" when I first started working with law enforcement trainers. The word meshes so perfectly with the purposeful mindset of Verbal Defense & Influence that I was hooked.

Tactical thinking is goal-driven and solution-oriented. Tactical thinking offers the sharpness of mind necessary to hone in on an issue and make things happen (at home as much as work).

Adopting a tactical approach brings levity and balance to situations because you remain focused on the issue at hand, instead of getting distracted or veering off in another direction. It pulls together some of the qualities we will be discussing throughout this chapter:

- A when-then mindset (from Chapter 1)
- An alert state of watchfulness
- An attitude of decisiveness
- A plan for responding

At home, next time you're locked in a stalemate conversation with your significant other, see what you get accomplished in a conversation that is directed by tactical thinking.

By focusing on the issue at hand you'll avoid the emotional landmines that cause drama, and work to achieve a clear-headed resolution.

For example: if you're discussing why the toilet seat is always up, keep it about the toilet seat. It's a simple problem that calls for a simple solution, right?

This shouldn't be the opportunity you seize to get nasty:

- *You never do what I ask you to do.*
- *You're a slob.*
- *Men are pigs.*

Yikes. See where this can go? Not a place I'd like to be. It's never a good idea to blow up small issues that do nothing but start wars between Venus and Mars.

The punch you should have heard

Conflicts start small, says Dave Young, a veteran police trainer and Vistelar's family safety and defense expert. Only in rare instances does violence occur without clear warning signs. When the warning signs are unaddressed, disregarded or ignored, the chances for deepening violence loom large.

"There is oftentimes a disrespectful tone of voice, a verbal confrontation or a push or shove that precede a punch in the face," said Young.

If we were to trace a violent act backwards, as the U.S. Department of Justice has done, we'd see that verbal disagreements were involved in 85.5 percent of all murders. Yes, the triggers that cause stress can escalate to extreme physical force.

We call these triggers "gateway behaviors" because, if left unchecked, they can easily escalate into more dangerous behaviors. Emotions, words and low-level behaviors like pushing are gateway behaviors to more physically violent actions.

Ask any teacher, nurse or police officer and they'll tell you how a conversation can escalate from mundane to urgent in the blink of an eye.

Conflict can escalate within our personal lives, too, and can have devastating results.

So it's good to know how to spot some of the warning signs: yelling, cursing, tense muscles, clenched fists and angry facial expressions.

Psychologists point out that, while strangers can make us angry, those closest to us have the ability to rile up our strongest emotions. According to anger expert Dr. Howard Kassinove:

"Interestingly, anger usually emerges from interactions with people we like or love, such as children, spouses and close friends."

Certainly, there is anger among strangers—getting skipped in line at the grocery store or cut off in traffic is infuriating. But step lightly and be prepared to de-escalate when these warning signs are present in the home: anger aimed at loved ones is what truly devastates.

LESSON 5: Learning to respond, not react

React and respond both describe the behavior that results after an occurrence, but connote very different outcomes.

In chemistry, a reaction takes place when you mix two substances together. It's instantaneous and inevitable as soon as the substances are put together. Likewise, a kneejerk reaction is the reflexive result of something happening to you.

A response, on the other hand, is user-driven. You choose how to respond to a situation. It is a decision, and you are in control. Police respond to an emergency. The student prepares a careful response to the teacher's question. A wise spouse responds to their partner's anger.

By learning how to suppress their gut-level reaction and project a more reasoned response instead, a young person, for example, can stay bully-proofed for life.

Sometimes children think they are being picked on because of the way they look (whether it's short, tall, fat or skinny). But that's not the case, according to Chan Lee, a martial arts master and Vistelar consultant who helped developed the company's anti-bullying materials for youth.

"Some people are targeted because they are sending out signals," said Lee. "The way they react to bullying sends out a signal that says 'bully me.'"

Sure, there might be a physical trigger that prompts the bullying to start. But, as not every freckle-faced redheaded child is bullied, there is something else making the target susceptible to victimization while others are not.

It's their response to *"Hey fatso,"* or *"Watch out, stupid"* that makes them vulnerable to further bullying. Bullying is rained upon kids who are emotionally gratifying to a bully.

A bully cannot torment someone who is unflappable.

And, while a child might not be able to control the trigger (shortness, nearsightedness, a family predisposition to Dr. Who), they have a measure of control over the way they behave.

They can choose to respond—and not react—to the bullying.
If they develop the ability to respond, they will have confidence that they can carry through life.

LESSON 6: Building decisiveness

When you are engaged in your interactions and your environment, you can be on the lookout for warning signs.

Functioning in an alert state of awareness lets you have enough facts to act decisively when the time comes.

But first, you must get familiar with the conditions before you can function properly.

You know how baseball has coaches posted at first and third base letting the runner know whether it's safe to run or not? Well, we don't have our personal base coaches perched on our shoulders in real life to tell us whether to stay or go. Acting decisively, therefore, is a quality that needs to come from within.

If you think back to situations that require you to move from the unknown to the known—adapting to a new job skill, figuring out the new user interface on your iPhone, getting acclimated to winter after the first snowfall—you can see that decisiveness develops only when you're familiar with the conditions.

When my son was learning to drive, he wasn't able to be decisive because he was not yet familiar with the conditions of driving.

As a student driver, he'd stop at a stop sign, look left, right and left again. Then he'd inch forward and repeat the process. By this point, the oncoming vehicle that had previously been a half-block away was now too close. So we'd stay stopped.

Aaagh!

Once that car had passed he'd start the process over again. Look left, right, left. Inch up. Left, right, left. It took forever before he would tentatively cross the road.

He had all the information he needed the first time he looked to proceed during his first window of opportunity. But the opportunity passed because he still wasn't able to process the information and move quickly enough.

It's gotten better, of course, as he's become more acquainted with both the conditions and the physical act of driving.

But it gave me a greater appreciation for the capacity to act decisively.

Here are a few tips for developing decisiveness:

1. Know what you wnt to get accomplished. Let's say you are a teacher and you want your student to put away his or her cell phone. Focus on the problem at hand. That is tactical thinking. (Resist the urge to embark upon your *"you-need-to-pay-more-attention"* speech.)

2. Know what your options are and determine the best way to get him to comply. You could walk up to him directly or address him in front of the group. You could take his phone away or ask him to put it in his backpack. Consider your options and make a decision.

3. Have a preplanned, practiced response. If you want the student to put down his or her cell phone, make sure you know—before you start to speak— how you would address his resistance. Ask yourself, *"What would I say if he doesn't put down the phone?"*

Your authority weakens when you appear wishy-washy.

Decisiveness is a quality that needs attention. There is no such thing as a third-base coach in life: there's no all-seeing guide who can watch your life on the sidelines and tell you whether to stay or run. Therefore, developing your personal capacity for tactical thinking is essential for becoming decisive.

Consider the triggers of others

Now that we have an idea of what's happening within us at the point of conflict, it's time to introduce the second great variable, the other person, into the equation.

The same triggers we discussed for ourselves are lurking and baiting the other person to snap, too.

For many of us who work in contact professions, we know to expect that on the job. People come to us in a compromised condition and at a heightened level of stress.

They're "under the influence"—and that doesn't just refer to substances, but also feelings, anger, stress, pain or fear.

But even if we deal with other people by day, we aren't always accepting of the fact that people back at home are just as vulnerable to such emotions and need to be managed well, too.

Part of managing ourselves involves sensitivity to the conditions of others. In other words, even if we're not bringing conflict to the table, we can find ourselves with a plateful of trouble anyway.

I'll use myself as an example. Once, when my husband came home after a lousy day at work, he just wanted to vent a little steam. I listened for a minute or so, then casually reached over and started checking texts and emails on my phone. Before long I was checking my friends on Facebook.

I was clearly ignoring him.

How rude of me. I never would have done that to a co-worker or client, but I did it to the man I love.

He got angry, I got defensive and his bad day—which I could have improved—poisoned our evening instead.

For these situations our trainers like to ask: what are you going to bring to the fire—gas or water?

I learned the hard way that insensitivity can be as flammable as gas.

CHAPTER 2 CHALLENGE

Now that you understand some strategies for reading situations and responding with appropriately, turn to the Communicating Under Pressure chart (page 12) to see how the following concepts fit in:

- Alert and decisive
- Respond, don't react

Answer the following questions:

1. What has been your approach to conflict in the past? Did you rush in? Leave? Act indecisively? Ignored the warning signs?
2. Recall an instance when you leapt to a conclusion without full knowledge of a situation.
3. How did you react?
4. Consider each of these concepts, and how they can improve your approach:
   - Tactical thinking
   - Being alert to the situation and to others
   - Responding, not reacting
   - Acting decisively
   - Recognizing the triggers of others

Chapter 3

Reframe your outlook:

How to show respect, even when it's hard

Overview: Your outlook drives your actions. And if your goal is to be effective in all of your encounters, your mission should be to treat people right.

In the midst of a disagreement, no one will budge from his or her viewpoint until there's movement toward common ground.

Until then, we're all stuck.

Unfortunately, we typically turn to our values to create our common ground—but that's oftentimes the source of our disagreement (if you've ever argued with someone else over politics you know what I mean). Either we don't know the other person's values or we consider them unreasonable.

Values don't solve our problems; it's unrealistic to think you can convert someone to your belief system or your set of values. They have their own, and they're entitled to them.

So how, then, do we move forward?

The promise of the book is a single, comprehensive framework for resolving conflict. We have to identify a quality that transcends values to move us toward common ground with someone else—even if that other person, compared to us, seems unreasonable, strange or wrong.

In our organization's 30+ years of teaching conflict resolution, only one concept has been robust enough to bridge these differences. Only one concept connects neighbors and friends, strangers and enemies, and those of different cultures, religions and ages.

In this chapter I'll break down the Verbal Defense & Influence guideposts. They are called the Five Maxims of Treating People with Dignity by Showing Them Respect.

I'll explain how these principles are used in professional applications to bring peace to volatile situations. And then I'll tell you where it's been most effective for me: in establishing a loving level of guidance with my children.

Defining dignity and respect

Because this chapter is all about leveraging what we all hold in common—the desire to be treated with dignity and shown respect—it's useful to qualify what is meant by these terms.

Treating people with dignity and showing them respect has been, until now, a process that has been rather loosely defined.

We all know we want it, but we fall short on how to pinpoint or deliver it.

Let's start by looking at dignity. What is it exactly? If an image of a butler with a white towel over his arm popped into your mind, you're not the only one who might rely on caricature.

We think about dignity in a situational context. We notice it in act— *"that was undignified"*—or in an appearance —*"he looks quite dignified."* We don't recognize it as a constant quality that needs affirmation.

Understanding the idea of respect is just as hazy. It's hard to define respect as an action verb. In fact, it's probably easier for you to recollect how angry you felt by being disrespected than it is to recall a time when you were shown respect.

Showing respect is more than just doing an act of respect. Offering a handshake is respectful in American culture, but just the gesture is not enough. It must be accompanied by an attitude that projects your desire to treat the other person right.

Unfortunately, when it comes to showing respect, we step lightly because we are afraid of how our actions might be misinterpreted: holding the door open for me might be an act of respect on your part, but I might interpret it and perceive it as a sign of sexism.

Because attempts to convey respect can be misinterpreted, we need a more robust interpretation of how we should treat people, one that is not wishy-washy or dependent on understanding someone's personal preferences. The interpretation that we've found successful is this:

All human beings, simply by virtue of being human, are deserving of a baseline of respect. We call that human dignity. When others violate that, whether through disregard, objectification, or by demeaning us, we are offended because a core part of who we are has been stripped away.

The Five Maxims provide tactic-driven strategies that let you, even in the midst of disagreement, move toward common ground. If you look at our Communicating Under Pressure chart (page 12), you'll see that the Five Maxims act as a frame that wraps around all of the skills we teach.

Before you can manage a situation, you need to be willing to acknowledge the dignity of others and be capable of treating them with respect.

LESSON 7: The Five Maxims of Treating People with Dignity by Showing Them Respect

The Five Maxims outline the action steps that need to be taken in order to show people respect in the times when they need it most:

1. Listen with all your senses
2. Ask, don't tell, others to do something
3. Explain why they are being asked
4. Offer options, not threats
5. Give them a second chance

The Maxims put our principles into action: acknowledging the dignity of another person and treating them with respect defines our outlook. The Maxims provide us with the how.

What you need is a willingness to acknowledge the dignity of others, the capacity to treat them with respect and the skills to manage the situation.

Our values set us apart (and that's OK)

We all know—and value—the things that set us apart. So it's only natural to expect some defensiveness and opposition when our choices fall into opposition.

Our choices reflect our values. Let's take food as an example.

If I'm a vegan and you love meat, us both sitting down and enjoying Thanksgiving dinner is going to require some special accommodations.

Now, food is an easy example of the value embedded in what seem like straightforward decisions that actually turn out to be triggers for conflict.

Move up the value chain and the potential for disagreement is even more ponderous: how you parent, whom you love, or what you worship.

You've got your own set of values, and so do I.

That's why treating people based upon dignity and respect, not upon whether you agree with their personal choices, is the best way to conduct interactions that leave everyone's dignity intact.

Moreover, this tactic leads to positive results.

Applying dignity and respect to parenting

One of the hardest parts of parenting teenagers is the process of gracefully detaching and granting them independence.

Some of us are better than others. I myself am a work in progress. As a mother accustomed to some measure of control, this process really stinks.

I'm loosening up the reins on my 16- and 14-year-old sons and my 11-year-old daughter, so they have the freedom to manage their choices— and sometimes, I need to let them make mistakes.

I used to be able to talk them out of impulse purchases, outrageous junk food and awful hairstyles, but not so much anymore.

Case in point: my older son has grown out his facial hair to the point that his friends started calling him "Wolverine." Yuck.

It is hard to sit on the sidelines and watch the parade of bad choices. It is also hard to walk the tightrope between granting them a measure of autonomy, while at the same time setting and enforcing strict rules.

Hair? Have it your way. Curfew? Mine.

Every day holds encounters that test my mettle: how do I respect their independence and guide them appropriately? Those are some pretty high stakes as we work our way through the stages of building maturity.

Here's an in-depth breakdown of how the Five Maxims have helped me through.

MAXIM 1. Listen with all your senses

Think of listening as an action sport. You're not just hearing; you're engaging all of your senses to ascertain the meaning.

You're listening, watching, observing and putting two-and-two together.

Ask any parent whose kid has broken curfew. That mother or father is not just listening to the words. They're using every single one of their senses (including gut intuition) to understand the situation and context.

They're listening for inconsistencies and they're trying to spot warning signs of trouble. They're also trying to get to the bottom of what really happened.

This process is called Beyond Active Listening, and we will cover it thoroughly in Chapter 6. In a nutshell this process details the action steps for actively engaging in fact-finding and understanding.

You can't just hear them; you've got to understand what they're saying. You ask questions, paraphrase, and summarize in order to understand how they see the situation, and then you use that information to work together in finding a solution. That's how you will inspire them to make better choices.

MAXIM 2. Ask, don't tell others, to do something

Consider the power of asking someone to do something instead of telling or directing them to do so. Achieving buy-in is a powerful persuasive technique.

Having a sense of ownership of the problem or issue gives people a sense of control over a seemingly impossible situation.

I know how tempting it is to rush in and play the Mom Card: it's my right to tell you what to do. But angry righteousness will put up an instant barrier between me and my 16-year-old.

Treating him with dignity by showing him respect means that my goal is more than simple compliance. The conversation is partly about being in by 11 p.m., but really, it's mostly about building a foundation of trust.

"Sean, what are some ways for not breaking curfew again?"

MAXIM 3. Explain why they are being asked

Explaining why they're being asked to do something gives the other person insight into the bigger picture.

If you think back to your own experiences, understanding the why is powerfully motivating. You understand how your actions play into the bigger picture.

You don't have to like the fact that, say, you have to leave a party when it's still in full swing, but knowing the why behind the act makes the need easier to understand.

So it's definitely important to offer some perspective to the people who matter most. In the case of the curfew there are multiple reasons they're being asked to get with the program:

- It's the law.
- It's our family agreement.

And most importantly:

- I want to trust you.

MAXIM 4. Offer options, not threats

For those of us in positions of authority or power, we know exactly where things can end up.

We can yank privileges, take away car keys and keep 'em grounded until next year. But instead of behaving like the wicked stepmother not letting

Cinderella go to the ball, we want others to have some choice in how they want the situation to end.

Options are empowering, while threats are demeaning.

Here's some advice for positioning options: you want to make your positive options as appealing as you can, and your negative ones vividly distasteful. You know what makes them tick (thanks to Maxim #1), and so you can use that to help persuade them gently.

Again, if the focus is on building trust, which statement is going to be more effective?

"Break curfew again and you're grounded."

or

"I know you want to keep going to parties. Can you keep better track of the time?"

Why not let the choice be theirs?

MAXIM 5. Give them a second chance

The second chance is an empowering tool. Granting someone a do-over lets them make good and maintains your authority.

This is an indispensable modus operandi for parenting teenagers and others who need support as they build their decision-making skills.

It also gives them a chance to slow down and think things through—both are greatly needed in the midst of conflict.

For this example, here's how I would embed the second chance into the summarizing piece of the listening sequence we described in Maxim 1:

"Sean, it sounds like you didn't notice until it was too late that your phone battery died and you lost track of the time.

"You said that you understand why you need to be in by 11.

"Because you appreciate the privilege of going out with your friends you said you will wear a watch and check the time more closely.

"I'll let you give that a try next Friday."

A second chance doesn't mean that there are no consequences. If my son had missed curfew before, he might have a shorter curfew this time. If he persistently violated curfew, I wouldn't hesitate to take away his late-night privileges. But before I become the disciplinarian, I want to make sure that I've given him an opportunity to regain my trust.

Maxims apply to all situations

Once you start using the Five Maxims to direct your interactions, you will start to key in and hear when it's being used all around you.

I'm sure you know people who seem plugged in and responsive to the needs of others. There's so much to be learned from them. In fact, I'm always learning and marveling at how people use this in every facet of life.

A few days ago I was in the office of my 14-year-old son's middle school, watching one of the office ladies, Ms. E.—a true master—in action. Ms. E. was dismissing a boy who was being sent home because of an angry outburst.

This had the potential to get ugly. The boy's dad walked in, and he looked angry too.

I watched Ms. E. take stock of the situation. She didn't get flustered, like many of us might have done. Instead, she stood a little straighter and gave them a warm smile—the very first indications that she would be showing them dignity by treating them with respect.

"Sam, you're a good boy," she said in a matter-of-fact tone. "We want you to get the most out of middle school, we want you to learn and make new friends. Can you try not to let your anger get the best of you?" (Recall Maxims 2 and 3, about explaining why, and asking rather than telling. These are powerful messages promoting buy-in.)

Before dismissing them both, Ms. E. added, "We're looking forward to having you back to school again tomorrow."

That was it. The boy and his father were able to leave the school with their dignity intact.

Ms. E. had gotten her message across: *You belong here. You made a mistake, but we want you back.*

As a witness to the situation I could think of countless tipping points when this conversation could have gone wrong, for the boy, the father and Ms. E. But she delivered exactly the message the boy and his dad needed to hear. The boy wasn't being blamed; he was being challenged to get better. And he was granted a second chance.

The Five Maxims in action are a beautiful, powerful thing.

Some final thoughts

Although we've been talking about the Five Maxims mostly within an interpersonal context, they were actually developed for professionals to manage conflict with people they didn't have a pre-existing relationship with to fall back on.

It was developed as a way of helping first responders and other emergency providers initiate contact and conduct themselves effectively, regardless of background of the people they served. This structure provided a template for agencies to implement a way to treat people right, no matter whom.

This outlook can be a game-changer, personally and professionally.

Let's take a look at the corporate world. So much professional training focuses on diversity, the wedges that set us apart (culture, gender, religion and race, to name a few). We value our distinctiveness, in the choices we make in life.

But in dignity and respect we stand united.

When it comes to what really matters, we're all playing on the same team. Once you make that realization, the whole game—your whole world—will change right before your eyes.

CHAPTER 3 CHALLENGE

Now that you understand how the Five Maxims can shape your outlook, turn to the Communicating Under Pressure chart (page 12) to see how the following concepts fit in.

Answer the following questions:

1. Reflect upon this statement: treating people with dignity by showing them respect makes others less resistant and you more effective. Have you ever considered the link between showing respect and eliminating resistance?

2. Consider a situation in your own experiences in which you were not treated with dignity or shown respect.

How would the outcome have changed if you were?

3. How do you relate the Five Maxims to interactions you have had, or plan to have?

Chapter 4

It's Showtime!

How to appear confident and capable

Overview: *What's Showtime? It's the best way to describe the mental and physical process of putting on and maintaining your game face.*

Up to this point, we've been talking about building your outlook and approach. Here is a roundup of some of the advances you've made so far:

- You accept conflict as a given.
- You know your triggers, and have discovered some strategies for how to master them.
- You are aware of situations, pay attention to the triggers of others and watch for budding signs of conflict.
- You are prepared to respond purposefully if you see a negative situation developing.

In the last chapter we introduced one of the concepts so fundamental to Verbal Defense & Influence that it drives all of our actions in the midst of stress.

This guiding principle is to treat others with dignity by showing them respect. Acting upon respect is not only the right thing to do; it also puts you on the fast track toward gaining buy-in.

If I step on my teenager's dignity during an argument, that's not going to move us toward resolution, will it? I need to act in a way that shows respect if I want to get through our short-term struggle in a way that doesn't endanger our long-term relationship.

I can't stress the importance of this in our personal lives. While people come and go in my professional life—co-workers move on, as do bosses—the people I encounter within my personal life seem to be here for good.

Even casual acquaintances can be around longer than I anticipated. I need to learn how to resolve my issues with my child's U6 soccer coach, because it's very likely that I will be encountering that person at school and community functions for a dozen years or so, until all of my kids graduate.

The reality is that you won't automatically get along with everyone who plays on your sports team, attends your church or volunteers with your community group. You need a way to break the chain of misunderstandings, squabbles and petty rivalries. You don't have to like the other person you're dealing with—but you do have to interact productively with them.

So far you've learned how to tune into the situation, have self-control over your triggers and now use the Five Maxims as a blueprint for treating people with dignity by showing them respect.

If I could picture you now, I'd see someone who aims to be at the top of his or her game. I'd see someone ready for a little Showtime.

This is the quality that will make you look, act and feel like a superstar.

The Showtime approach

The concept of Showtime meshes together all of the physical and mental preparedness you need to take into the situation.
Displaying a polished persona is what separates the pros from the amateurs.

"Does a professional ever look like he or she is having a bad day? Of course not," said Gary T. Klugiewicz, head trainer for Verbal Defense & Influence.

"Do professionals have bad days? Of course they do," he said. "They just don't show it."

Showtime is a professional mindset, and that extends into whatever you happen to be doing. Skillful, proficient and capable are words that don't just pertain to your day job. Showtime lets you put these qualities on display, no matter what you do.

But how do we go about showing off what it means to be our best?

I'll start off with a little story about what it looks like to witness this transition into Showtime.

It's not magic, really

My 16-year-old son landed his first job a few months ago, performing table magic for family nights at a local restaurant.

Tuesday afternoons when he comes home from school, he stashes away his backpack and begins to peel back his everyday layers.

He carefully irons a button-up shirt, and pairs it with suspenders and a bow tie. He puts on a vest and a blazer.

He packs his pockets with his work supplies—decks of cards, invisible thread and foam balls. Right before he leaves, he gels his hair and studies himself in the mirror.

The metamorphosis is complete. He has become an illusionist, one who now only vaguely resembles the kid who lives with us.

Our daily transformation

The process isn't much different than the one we all go through before we punch in for the day. We dress the part, whether we're putting on the company polo shirt and khaki pants or a business suit and wing tips. Our clothes reflect who we are professionally.

Certainly, these physical trappings mean something to us. It's equally worthwhile to point out that our appearance makes a difference to others, too. Wearing a uniform sends out a signal that your persona has become more than it was before.

Why is that? Because you now have extra qualities infused into the presence you project. The knowledge you possess, your expertise and your experience are all on display because your appearance has been embedded with meaning.

If we were to meet one another on the street, you wouldn't have a built-in expectation that I could advise you on your next computer purchase—but if I were wearing a bright blue Best Buy shirt you could reasonably have that expectation. Even if I'm nowhere near the store, you can tell that I represent the company.

My shirt connects me to Best Buy in a visual way that anyone can see. So my behavior and appearance reflect not only upon me, but upon the company that I represent.

But there are other qualities that can telegraph my authority and project professional competence:

- Confident nonverbal body language, such as a strong posture without slumped shoulders or crossed arms.
- Good eye contact that establishes a personal connection.
- Alertness so that I am tuned into my surroundings.
- Approachability so that I look ready to assist others.

All of these elements together—the whole package of appearing professional, competent and confident—comprise what we call your "professional face." Your professional face is what you wear to project confidence. It doesn't matter whether you're the one in charge or not; you look the part.

By contrast, your "personal face" is how you show yourself when you let your guard down. This is the side of you that gets tired, emotional, angry or vulnerable. You should display your personal face only under the most secure conditions.

Developing Showtime: What's happening physically?

When you put on a uniform or style of dress, others expect you to operate at a different level of professionalism and competence.

Those elevated expectations skyrocket if you are someone who operates within the public trust. Want to hush a room? Wear your military dress uniform (or a Roman collar, for that matter) and all eyes will be watching what you do.

Our Verbal Defense & Influence trainers work with groups to build an understanding of the art of representation, that people's perception of us changes when we display what and whom we represent.

It's easy to picture the physical qualities of professionalism when you're talking about someone wearing a uniform, which is why I started out with this strong mental image.

These qualities shine through and reinforce your commitment. Projecting a powerful presence shouldn't just be relegated to your work hours; your best presence matters in community and personal life, too.

LESSON 8: Showtime on display

Here are some techniques for Showtime behavior to engage your professional face when you're heading into a situation (especially one that has the potential for conflict):

- Stack your blocks. Plant your feet and stack your body from a grounded position so that your feet, knees, hips, back, chest, neck, and head are all aligned.
- Say *"It's Showtime!"* Taking a moment to check yourself in the mirror and whisper, *"It's Showtime"* strengthens your connection to the specific behaviors that you associate with Showtime.
- Breathe: Take some deep breaths to help mange your physiological reaction to stress. Stress disrupts our breathing, thereby cutting oxygen off to the brain. You need to consciously breathe deeply and soon, this will become your practiced response.
- Balance: Settle in to lower and stabilize your center of balance, relax your hips, soften your knees and place your fleet flat on the floor. Roll your shoulder blades up, back and down and stand straight, not tipped forward. Remember you're operating with a when-then mentality that keeps you prepared for the unexpected—so be ready to respond.
- Positive self-talk: Tell yourself what you already know: *"I can handle this."*

LESSON 9: Priming strategies

In a popular TED Talk from 2012, social psychologist Amy Cuddy spoke on the topic of body language and power. Her laboratory experiments reveal that spending two minutes "power posing"—standing with your feet shoulder-width apart, your hands on your hips and your chin up—promotes a rise in the power hormone testosterone and a decrease in the stress hormone cortisol.

"When you pretend to be powerful you are more likely to actually feel powerful," she said.

Indeed, you can configure your brain to achieve personal power. Don't just fake it until you make it. "You can fake it 'til you become it," Cuddy said.

This technique isn't just for adults; it works for youth, too. Quick example: I coach forensics and public speaking at the middle school. Before the first meet of the year, I taught to one of my new students, Ian, how to "stack his blocks." (He recognized it as a stance he learned in wrestling, and he called it head-over-heart-over-hips.)

That following week, he told me this posture made all the difference in calming his nerves and establishing his presence. Did I mention Ian won a first place trophy at the last meet and is advancing to state?

Having a greater awareness that recognizes the touchpoints of the change from personal face to professional face is what neuroscientists refer to as "self-priming." If you wink at the mirror, put on your ID lanyard, and whisper, "It's Showtime," you're forming a mental association.

Gestures like that aren't as crazy as they sound; sports teams often go through pregame rituals that get players pumped for the upcoming game. In fact, do a Google search for "best pregame rituals" and you'll see lots of outrageous behaviors and superstitions of professional athletes. Whatever the specific action is, it sets them up for the game ahead.

One of our consultants has even posted a Communicating Under Pressure chart (page 12) to his refrigerator—it's his reminder that the folks at home deserve a little of his Showtime, too.

Making it through your bad days

You've had bad days before and you'll have them again. But they don't need to control you, said Vistelar consultant Bob "Coach" Lindsey, 2013 International Law Enforcement Educators and Trainers Association Trainer of the Year. Bad days put us at heightened risk for conflict, which is why he recommends an approach grounded in Showtime.

It's useful to acknowledge and accept the fact that you are having a bad day, he said. Then, engage in the Showtime steps from Lesson 8. They help reset you both in mind and body.

"Transcend the bad day," Lindsey says. "Others around you don't know you are having a bad day; therefore, you must perform."

Monitor your attitude and remember: respond, don't react, to situations.

"Since I've started doing this the moments in my bad days are getting less and less, and they have less effect," he said. "I don't let the circumstance, the stimulus or the mood control me.

"I've discovered that we all have the power to become better."

Some Frequently Asked Questions about Showtime

Put my best face forward? How hard is that? It is tempting to be dismissive of what may seem like a straightforward concept, but there are more moving parts than you might realize.

Q: When do I need to say *"It's Showtime?"*
When you least feel like it. Seriously.

It's easy for me to be a stellar parent on the days when my kids are outstanding, when they're courteous to strangers and when they are kind to one another.

It's harder to get my game on when they are acting up, mouthing off and picking fights. The same thing is true at work: when my co-workers annoy me, cut me down or just don't listen, I struggle to be my best.

It's so easy to react with that primal part of my brain. This boiling point is when Showtime is so crucial, because that nanosecond pause gives my reasoned brain a chance to respond.

I've coined a new phrase for the words that result from the heat of the moment: I call it lizard language, the slimy byproduct of our reptilian brain.

On the bad days, adopting a Showtime mindset makes us capable of letting our language catch up with our true brains. It's the pause that refreshes. It gives us the capability to respond, not react.

Q: Is this the same as being nice?

Not at all. The urge to be accepted and liked puts roadblocks on the road to professionalism, because the act of being professional requires an openness to making tough—i.e., unpopular—choices.

Last year our team worked with animal inspectors from the U.S. Department of Agriculture's Horse Protection Agency. The group monitors horse shows to make sure that none of the trainers engage in cruel or abusive training practices.

These veterinarians, who are all supporters by nature, are thrust in the awkward position of enforcing lawful standards of care in an intense, high-stakes environment.

For supportive people who have the best interest of the horses at heart, it's tough to acknowledge the reality that their good work and best intentions will meet with resistance.

It's not so different than what teachers encounter in a classroom.

"The desire to be popular is common among young and inexperienced teachers," said Danielle Shryock, a veteran middle school teacher who uses Verbal Defense & Influence in the classroom.

The desire to be liked leads to inconsistency in the classroom policy and gaps in your professionalism. A teacher whose primary impulse is to be liked by students is leading from insecurity, not confidence.

Danielle takes great pride in knowing that she is respected by her students—whether they like her or not.

Remember: the goal is to appear confident. You can do that while being friendly in many circumstances, but don't lose sight of the goal.

Q: When can I turn off the Showtime?

Not until you're off duty—and that includes off duty from your family, too. Sure, you've been plugged in and engaged all day, and you've been the epitome of professional. By the time you clock out and head home you're ready to change into sweatpants, watch TV and pop a cold one.

It's exhausting to be the fire putter-outer, the clear-headed thinker, responsive to the needs of others and committed to the tasks of the day.

You deserve a break, but your kid/spouse/lover/BFF deserves a little quality time. What do you do?

The moment you turn the handle and open the door could be the most critical point of your day, more important than anything that happened at work.

You look around and spend five minutes engaging. Smile and make eye contact. Have a pleasant conversation. If you fall off the rails, use our framework for communicating under pressure, which lets you hop back on track.

It's an unrealistic expectation that, at the end of a bad day, you'll be set and ready for sustained quality time with your family. But you should be able to maintain your composure long enough to check in before you decompress.

Keep the reptilian part of your brain in check and don't unleash the lizard language. These are the people that matter most in your world.

Showtime will get you through those first few critical minutes back at home, when the risk is high that your professional face will come off with a thud.

Control your stress so that the people you most care about get the best you can give at 6:00 p.m.

Q: Isn't this a phony construct?

No. You're simply displaying a better version of you.

It's been said that tactics such as Showtime are like putting on an act, one that serves to shield and hide your authentic self from the world.

Sorry, I don't buy that. Even if you choose to keep your professional and personal worlds well separated, your personal integrity plays a major role in your professional presence. There's nothing fake about it.

The personal and professional you don't exist on separate planets. If you can't make your professional life align with your persona, unless you are an actor, you may be in a line of work inappropriate for your whole self. In other words, Showtime is like putting on your Sunday best—it's not the costume of a completely different person.

Q: Does this apply to kids?

You bet. Being able to manage the image they project is fundamental to both building confidence and steering bullies away. While a child might think they are targeted because of a certain physical or personal quality, they are really bullied because their reaction somehow gratifies the bully.

Remember, bullies select their prey much like a lion chooses a slow-moving animal. Likewise, a bully targets a child who can be taken down and made low.

Teaching them to manage their gut-level reaction and put on a professional face provides the opportunity to consider their nonverbal language and the image they project, as well as their emotions when under stress.

For all of us, being able to control our reactions is the first step to being in control around others and in stressful situations. It's as applicable for them on the playground as it is for you in your own world.

Some final thoughts

Appearances count, and you have the ability to manage yours in the moments that matter.

The presence you project reflects upon those whom you serve and those whom you represent, especially if you're driving the company van or wearing the company t-shirt.

But whom do you really represent? That's a much deeper issue.

One of our trainers, Peter Harrell, Jr., asked an interesting question: "If you made the news today, who would be proud (or upset) for what you did?"

The list would include your family, your friends and maybe your neighbors. You'd be surprised at all the people who would come out of the woodwork. We don't always realize how many people have stake in the image we present.

So stack your blocks, smile and be ready for Showtime.

CHAPTER 4 CHALLENGE

Using what you've learned about Showtime, consider these questions. Turn to the Communicating Under Pressure chart (page 12) to see how the following concepts fit in.

1. Briefly describe your:
   - Professional face
   - Personal face
   - Who sees them, and when?
2. Describe your transition from private to professional—how well do you pay attention to the transformation in appearance and mindset? How do you stay composed (using your professional face), even in personal situations?
3. Name two physical and mental techniques for Showtime that you plan to use now.
4. What are some ideas you have for using Showtime at home?
5. Do you know a youth who could benefit from understanding this Showtime mindset? What principles will you share with them?

Chapter 5

Start off right:

How to master first impressions

Overview: How do you get your interaction started the right way? Thanks to Showtime, you've got the look. Now the Universal Greeting provides a template for knowing what to say.

First impressions set the tone for an interaction. This is the best time to build rapport and establish credibility and best yet, eliminate resistance.

We've already covered the importance of Showtime—by putting on your professional face, you project decisiveness and assertiveness. That's a great start.

Now we'll learn the Universal Greeting, so you don't lose precious time by fumbling around for what to say.

It may seem as if some people, more than others, have a knack for approaching someone and starting a purposeful conversation. But it's more than a knack: it's a learnable, do-able skill for anyone (even if you're shy or you sometimes feel like you're at a loss for words when under pressure).

The Universal Greeting is as important to our Verbal Defense & Influence methodology as the Five Maxims and Showtime. Guiding and directing an initial interaction with someone, whether you know them or not, is as important as how you look and how you treat people.

"We have this default assumption that professional people know how to talk to each other, but they don't," said Tony Pinelle, a Verbal Defense & Influence consultant who specializes in teaching contact professionals like utility workers, mental health care professionals and others who are often on the receiving end of anger or hostility.

If Tony thinks this is a problem among contact professionals, I would bet that regular folks like you and I could stand some improvement, too.

Having a scripted approach—yes, your own personal spiel—gives you a launching point that is consistently effective. The Universal Greeting is a powerful script that can shut down conflict before it starts.

How does it work? Let me tell you a story about how a simple Universal Greeting helped me keep my cool.

It was a cold day...

It was an unseasonably cold winter, one that started a month early and caught everyone by surprise. Our furnace wasn't keeping up with the cold, and I was glad that I had made my appointment to get it serviced well in advance.

When the day came, it was five degrees and the wind felt as if it was chewing through the walls. I was bundled up as if I should have been at a football game and not at my desk. I had just one more hour left until the repairman was scheduled to arrive.

Then the phone rang.

"Good morning, this is Mary from Tom's Heating Service, here with a service update," said the voice of the scheduler. *"Am I speaking with Kathy? We just got a call from a woman whose 86-year-old mother is without heat today.*

"We would like to fix her situation before coming to you," she continued. *"Would you mind terribly if we pushed back your appointment an hour or so?"*

Did I mind? Not a bit. How noble of me to do the right thing. I hung up the phone and matter-of-factly rearranged my plans to accommodate this wrinkle in my schedule.

What happened here? On the surface, not very much. This encounter was agreeable enough, despite having created a minor inconvenience to my day. No big deal.

But let's consider what could have happened if that scheduler weren't as graceful. What if she would have said, *"This is Tom's Heating Service, informing you that your appointment has been pushed back to later this morning. Have a good day."* Click.

That one phone call from the heating company could have prompted me to react negatively, in which case I would have made the situation worse, for the caller and for the repairman once he got here.

But it didn't, and that's the beauty of the Universal Greeting.

Lesson 10: The Universal Greeting

As its name implies, the Universal Greeting is a launching technique for efficiently starting an interaction. This scripted response covers all your bases and lets you get to your point quickly.

There are four parts to the introduction; every one of them is designed to lay the foundation for the interaction.

The purpose is to let you state your business, circumvent resistance and give them the opportunity to start talking to you. This will clearly demonstrate your respect for them.

1. **Appropriate greeting:** Use the greeting that suits you best and use their name, if they are familiar to you.
   "Good morning!"
   While you could say "Hi" or "Howdy," we find that the slightly more formal salutation is a springboard for our Showtime presence.
2. **Identify yourself and your affiliation:**
   "This is Mary from Tom's Heating Service, here with a service update."
3. **Explain the reason for the contact:**
   "We just got a call from a woman whose 86-year-old mother is without heat today. We would like to fix her situation before coming to you."
4. **Ask a relevant question:**
   "Could we push back your appointment an hour or so?"
   In less than 10 seconds, both the sender and the receiver are

aligned and ready to carry on the conversation.

Starting off right

Is this small stuff? No, it's actually a pretty big deal. Here's why: it's as easy for me to snap at these meaningless, micro-encounters as it is for the more impactful ones.

Put it this way: if I'm capable of pitching a fit at some faceless scheduler, just think of the damage I can do (and have done) when I've disagreed with my child's teacher over something quite small, or escalated a tense conversation with the guy at work who I really don't like. Little things matter in setting the tone.

Such bad vibes can start the moment one of us walks into the room, and unless they can be defused, they grow from there.

That one phone call from the heating company could have turned my day in the wrong direction. But it didn't.

We don't always recognize those sterling moments when everything goes right, and therefore nothing happens at all. Having your own Universal Greeting makes them possible, and makes you aware of your capability to do things right.

His presumptions, my panic

What happens when you initiate a conversation with only a vague plan for what you need to accomplish? Let me give you a short example:

The phone rings and I answer.

Brad: *"Hello, this is Brad Higgins."*

Kathy: "(long pause) *Oh, you mean Mr. Higgins?* (another long pause as I scramble to make connections) *Dan's...math teacher?"*

Brad: *"Yes. How are you doing?"*

Kathy: "(uneasy) *Is everything OK?"*

Sure everything is fine and Mr. Higgins was just calling to update me on the school's upcoming math fair. But why didn't he say so?

This conversation wasn't launched in a way that set the tone or primed me to be responsive. I had to work at becoming receptive to him and his message.

In his training, Gary T. Klugiewicz says that our interactions set up two types of atmospheres, either supportive or defensive. I was definitely feeling defensive by this point.

Here's why: Brad plunged into the call with a mindset based on some shaky presumptions:

1. That I knew his first name (oftentimes, parents just don't).
2. That I connected him with Dan, and with math (three children times seven subjects apiece equals…a lot of teachers per semester).
3. That my first response, when hearing from a teacher, wouldn't be panic.

I know it's irrational, but seeing the school number on my caller ID plants the seeds of dread. I fear something has gone wrong.

It doesn't matter how well-performing my kids are in school. All kinds of worst-case scenarios live in this mother's anxiety closet: bad grades, fights and accidents in every shape, size and shade of intensity.

So I've spent 20 seconds dwelling in uncertainty, trying to suppress irrational anxiety, figure out who the heck is calling, and why.

What's happening on his end of the line isn't much better. He's probably wondering why I'm so uptight. But he shrugs it off, delivers his information and moves on to the next call.

Rote interactions like this get the tasks done but, if he continued to receive stand-offish responses from other parents, he probably chalked it up to a greater disconnect between parents and teachers. If he wasn't jaded yet, these calls might have moved him, however slightly, down that path.

But what if this teacher—and all of us who must work with others— viewed these initial moments of contact not as drudgery, but as opportunities to improve relationships and better solidify our position of competence and authority?

It wouldn't have taken much:

Greeting: *"Good morning Ms. Mangold."*

Identification: *"This is Brad Higgins, Dan's math teacher."*

Reason for contact: *"I wanted to take the opportunity to touch base and remind you of Thursday's math fair."*

Relevant question: *"Would you be able to volunteer for an hour?"*

The Universal Greeting structure is great because it wouldn't be hard for Mr. Higgins to modify it for those times when he's calling to tell me Dan forgot his homework, or was horsing around in class.

Here's how it could change:

Reason for contact: *"I thought you'd want to know that Dan forgot his homework for the third time this week."*

Relevant question: *"Is there something that's changed in his routine? It's unusual for him to neglect his work."*

The structure is in place to set up a supportive atmosphere, even if the message might not be something a parent wants to hear.

Lesson 11 : Customizing your own Universal Greeting

Being personable, while at the same time effectively setting up an interaction, are all teachable skills.

Picture the Universal Greeting as the key that opens the doors, whether you are in sales, the corporate world or interviewing for a job. You'll be protected from that uncomfortable feeling of being at a loss for words.

And yet so many of us avoid devising a script for an initial contact as if it's a pickup line to use at a bar. But knowing what you're going to say and then saying it well exudes confidence, whether you are networking at a business event…or selling Girl Scout cookies.

Sign me up for 10 boxes of Thin Mints next time the doorbell rings and I hear this, instead of a meek and uninspired, "Wanna buy some cookies?"

"Good morning, my name is Maria and I'm a Brownie with Troop 47 from Madison Elementary.

"I'm here today to see if you would like to purchase some delicious cookies and support Girl Scouts too.

"Could you take a look at my order sheet?"

More about youth

You can't be too young to learn the key to positive initial interactions. This is the best way to start speaking up for yourself and put assertiveness into practice.

It's intimidating to muster up the nerve and approach a teacher, especially if you're struggling in class or you need to share news that is difficult or unpleasant.

So what do kids say? In most cases they don't say anything at all. They just don't know where to start.

A Universal Greeting can guide their words and focus their purpose:

Greet and identify yourself: *"Hello Mr. Barnes, I'm Dan, from your fifth hour geometry class."*

Explain the reason for contact: *"The reason I'm here is to see if you can look over problems 5 and 6 from last night's homework.*

"I got them wrong and don't understand why."

Ask a relevant question: *"Can you help me with this now or should I come back after school?"*

Parents, you can't underestimate the importance of giving children the tools they need to speak up for themselves. And if you spend some time prepping these techniques with your child the night before, you have the added bonus of applying them tomorrow in your workplace interactions, too.

While you're at it go ahead and ask for that raise:

"Good morning, Boss.

"As you know, it's time to have my annual performance review.

"This seems like a good opportunity to discuss some salary issues I'd like to address.

"Is this a convenient time or should we schedule a meeting later today?"

You won't be winging it—you have the script right in front of you.

CHAPTER 5 CHALLENGE

Turn to the Communicating Under Pressure chart (page 12) and to see how the Universal Greeting covered in Chapter Five fits in.

1. Briefly summarize your thoughts on how the Universal Greeting addresses the following:
   - Managing your first impression
   - Effectively initiating a conversation
   - Building assertiveness
   - Shutting down negativity and resistance
   - Engaging consistently in all your interactions
2. How can you use Universal Greetings in your own life?
3. Create 1-2 Universal Greetings based on the following template:
   a. Greet and identify yourself
   b. Explain the reason for the contact
   c. Ask a relevant question
   d. Do you know others who would benefit from employing a Universal Greeting? Who?

Chapter 6

Check for understanding:

How to go Beyond Active Listening

Overview: You can't just hear another person; you've got to understand what they're saying. Empathy will help you inspire them to make better choices.

Eskimos have something like 50 different words for snow. We should have that many words in English for the nuanced word "listening" and its many layers of meaning.

For our purposes, the listening skill we are focusing on—listening in the midst of crisis—should generate understanding and set a course of action.

Listening for comprehension—a process we call Beyond Active Listening—is an all-engaging activity to inspire buy-in and action.

The challenge? Understanding the other person well enough to direct their desires to align with your intentions.

This type of listening is purpose-driven or, to use my favorite word, this approach to listening must be tactical.

Recapping what we've learned

This chapter marks a transition in our focus. Up to this point we've covered the proactive measures to put in place, everything from your outlook to your approach to your initial contact in instances where there is the potential for conflict.

You know how to prepare to enter the encounter using the right words and putting your best face forward.

Now we are going to make the shift to building a responsive skill set, learning how to respond to the words and actions of another.

For the purpose of conflict resolution and communicating under pressure, our focus is on purposeful listening to another person: listening with the objective of finding a resolution so we can move ahead together.

Beyond Active Listening is fundamental to Verbal Defense & Influence; this core skill ranks up there with Showtime, the Five Maxims and the Universal Greeting. You cannot function adequately in conflict without it.

In today's time of sensory overload, Beyond Active Listening is a whopper of a skill. The ability to tune in, pay attention and assimilate information is a priceless quality.

But it seems to me that it is increasingly more and more difficult to sustain.

We've grown accustomed to information coming at us like bullets; we're barraged with pings, tweets, alerts and instant messages.

Speaking for myself, as I've become more immersed in technology—particularly my cell phone—my ability to detach from such rapid-fire distractions and focus on the moment seems to be slipping away.

The moment you stop listening is the moment that gets you in trouble.

Building buy-in

The best way to maneuver your way through conflict is by practicing Beyond Active Listening.

If there's conflict, the other person has a different interest in the situation than you do. You can resolve this in several different ways—on a good day you can achieve agreement and partnership; on a bad day, attaining simple compliance might be a victory.

Here are some ways to define these various levels of buy-in:

- Compliance: enforcing the established rules and procedures.
- Cooperation: willingly working together to accomplish a task or goal.

- Collaboration: the best-case scenario, in which everyone is vested and committed to both the process and the outcome as partners.

Such purpose-driven listening is active, to say the least; Beyond Active Listening is the tool for moving them from where they are to where we want them to be.

Now, the concept of "active listening" has been around for a long time in communication training circles and basically means turning on the ears and moving from the passive act of hearing toward one of acknowledging what is being said.

In this chapter we will cover what you need to go Beyond Active Listening:

- Empathizing: Seeking to understand the perspective of another.
- Asking to clarify: Using questions to better understand where they're coming from.
- Paraphrasing: Using your words to reframe the issue
- Summarizing and moving ahead: Not wrapping things up until you've planned out your further course of action.

Wrong kind of listening gets me in trouble

We've all learned the physical signs that make it look like we're listening—acknowledging, taking notes, looking interested and making eye contact.

It's so easy to look as if I'm listening that I sometimes find myself play-acting rather than really listening. Earlier in the book I mentioned how frustrating it was for my husband when I was "listening" to him, but then slipped, forgot and started checking Facebook on my iPhone instead.

I'm sorry to say this had been an ongoing issue for me; I'm easily distracted and my inability to focus is a source of ongoing conflict—my husband, kids and parents all translate my fake listening as a sign of disrespect. (And I must admit, indeed it is.)

That's why the act of listening needs to go beyond displaying those outward appearances that don't truly translate into active engagement.

For distracted people like me, Beyond Active Listening lays out the steps I need to take to keep my attention from wandering. It's a matter of honing in, processing all sensory input, realizing what these messages mean and determining a course of action.

Listening with all your senses — and intuition

Watching a crime show will reveal this piece of truth: If Columbo or any other TV detective just relied on his ears he'd miss half of the hints being dropped all around him.

There are five senses, hearing, sight, smell, touch and taste. Observing, making note and deploying the sensory knowledge that you have gathered is incredibly effective.

This sixth sense is our instinct, and this is a sense worth developing and listening to.

The bad news, however, is that we try and squelch this sixth sense, because our gut instinct is something that cannot be explained through reason. But it's worthwhile to acknowledge that on a visceral level, our bodies and minds can sense when something is wrong.

"You have the gift of a brilliant internal guardian that stands ready to warn you of hazards and guide you through risky situations," says Gavin De Becker, author of The Gift of Fear.

Acknowledging and respecting our intuition helps us use Beyond Active Listening to tune in to danger and threat.

Lesson 12: Listen and build empathy

Because your focus is on understanding, you need to engage in projecting empathy. Verbal Defense & Influence instructor Kenneth Cook summed up the empathy-building process so succinctly when he said:

"You need to find a way to make their wants match your objectives."

It should be mentioned that Cook works as a jailer in Laramie County, Wyo.—his clientele is a population notorious for resistance and pushback. But he's cracked the universal code in neutralizing negativity and prompting people into positive action.

How do you start to identify their wants, particularly when you are dealing with people whose desires seem so far from your objectives?

By engaging in Beyond Active Listening, of course.

That applies whether you're dealing with inmates, middle schoolers or anyone in between.

LESSON 13: Responding with empathy

The first step in Beyond Active Listening is to project empathy. The quality of empathy is sometimes tricky for people to understand because it gets confused with sympathy. To state it simply, here's the difference between sympathy and empathy: empathy is an action, and sympathy is a feeling.

Empathy is what brings you to someone's level, trying to understand how the world looks through their eyes. Sympathy, on the other hand, will have you weeping in the corner.

Here are some suggestions that Verbal Defense & Influence consultant Doug Lynch, had for engaging your capacity for empathy:

1. We usually say to ourselves, *"I think the person sees..."* It is better to say to ourselves, *"The person seems to see..."* Consciously be aware of the assumptions and experiences you bring to the table, and work to more clearly see through the other person's eyes.

2. Look the person in the eyes. This is a powerful tool not just for having a person connect with us but also for us to connect with them.

3. Remember they are human and so are you.

4. Expand your horizons constantly. This is an ongoing process. The more knowledge we have of people, and the more knowledge we have of other cultures, the better we will relate to our fellow human beings.

Empathy is the ability to recognize the feelings and emotional state of others. When you project empathy you increase the odds that others will respond to you favorably.

One of the major discoveries in the field of neuroscience has been the mirror neuron response, which offers a scientific basis for the connection that we feel to the experiences of another.

"It seems we're wired to see other people as similar to us, rather than different," says neuroscientist and researcher Vittorio Gallese, MD, PhD, in an article by the American Psychological Association. "At the root, as humans we identify the person we're facing as someone like ourselves."

Now let's pause for a second here. This isn't the first time within the book that you're reading about congruence—recall the Five Maxims.

The thing we all hold in common is our desire to be treated with dignity by being shown respect. If you treat me empathetically you fulfill my desire to be respected.

If you treat me well, I'm more likely to treat you well in return. That's a simple truth, and neuroscience is just beginning to recognize its power.

Lesson 14: Mastering the art of clarification

Here's a fact that you probably already know (but sometimes forget): when people are in the midst of stress or conflict, they don't always say what they mean.

Their emotions color their words in various shades of rage, angst or anxiety. This mental shutdown happens to the best of us—in the thick of the moment, even the most articulate of us don't express ourselves as we should.

For the listener, these angry words feel like a slap to the ear. So we might be tempted to react to those words.

By now you know a better tactic: respond, don't react. So instead of snapping back at them, mirroring their same language and intensity, you need to remember to take a breath, calm yourself and consider where they're coming from (that's building empathy, the first strategy of Beyond Active Listening) and realize that they probably don't mean what they say.

Then, proceed with the second strategy of Beyond Active Listening, called Ask to Clarify.

You want to ask questions that help you understand their point. The questions can be anything from restating their concern—*"I never take responsibility around here? Is that what you believe?"* to *"Why do you say I never take responsibility?"* or *"I can tell you're upset. What's really going on here?"*

Get the idea?

By paying attention to what they're telling you, then asking followup questions to make sure you understand, you are able to get to the heart of the matter.

For example, *"You never take responsibility around here,"* probably boils down to, *"You forgot to feed the dog again."*

"Your cooking stinks," might just mean, *"Hey, you burned the chicken again."*

"I can't count on you for anything," is more like, *"You forgot to call me today."*

The good news is that once you determine the real cause of the problem, it's often actionable and solvable—*"Darnit that's right, I forgot to feed Alfie. why don't I set up an alert on my phone so I won't forget again?"*

Be careful not to get defensive, because that's also a reptilian response like that primal, lizard language. If you can stay calm and seek to understand, things are never as bad as it first may seem.

Or even if they are really bad (poor Alfie), you can't start a productive discussion until the anger is out of the air. You might need to follow up:

"You shouldn't have to bear all the responsibility for the dog, but I do have a problem remembering his mealtime. Let me think it over for a bit, but let's talk later today about improving the way we divide responsibilities."

You've bought yourself some time, and you're presenting them with the option to help achieve a solution.

Intelligence gathering is an art

The art of asking the right questions is such a good strategy that we shouldn't just save it for urgent situations. It's always good to have information in your back pocket, even when there's no threat of conflict.

You just need to know how to troll for information.

Driving a carpool of kids back and forth to school gave me the perfect opportunity to gather intel. But they are notoriously tough nuts to crack.

I asked them slightly amusing and occasionally disarming questions, followed up with an *"Oh yeah? Tell me more..."* Those van rides were chatty and informative.

- *"What was the best part of your lunch?"*
- *"Describe your teacher's jewelry today."*
- *"Name three things that happened to you."*
- *"What was the worst thing you learned?"*
- *"Did anyone chase you at recess?"*
- *"Did anyone throw up at school?"*

If I'd have just asked, "How was school today?" the answers would have been the typical grunts and eye rolls.

But that first question, a volley into their court, instead prompted them to retrace their steps through their day. Once they were back in school mode, they were mine. I could ask them anything I wanted to:

- Information-seeking questions should do just that— facilitate the other person's ability to step back into the situation and revisit their experiences. It's hard to reconstruct the details once a situation has passed; recalling specifics helps trigger a person's memory.
- Open-ended questions, like *"How was school today?"*—require more than a yes or no response. They encourage others to share not just information but also their viewpoint. But, they are only effective once the person has opened up and is ready to talk.
- Opinion-seeking questions, like *"How did you feel about that?"* show that you are empathetic to their feelings.
- Direct questions require a simple yes or no. The trick is to follow up with other questions that dig deeper into the issue:
  - *"Did you do well in your geometry test? No?"*
  - *"How did you prepare for it?"* (information-seeking)
  - *"What will you do differently next time?"* (open-ended).

Lesson 15: How to paraphrase

The process of comprehension needs to happen in real time—otherwise you leave the conversation confused and uncertain. Paraphrasing is a tool to help you make sure you understand a person's situation or viewpoint before it's too late.

Too bad there's not a Google Translate feature for speaking child (or in-law, or ex-spouse). They sprechen their message in their own code, and it's up to you to make sense of it.

You have two choices: to dig in and try and figure it out, or to bury your head in the sand and avoid confrontation.

If you're not sure where to begin synthesizing all the information and emotions that are swirling about, consider this simple formula:

"You're feeling X because of Y. Is that true?"

Enlisting their support by using a phrase like, "Help me understand…" extends the olive branch of empathy. And fortunately, they're going to be so eager to make sure you get their message that they'll stop venting/ranting/raging long enough for you to get it right.

"Help me understand—you believe that I don't like your friends because I won't let you go to the mall with them on Saturday? Is that correct?"

"In other words, you think I'm a lousy cook because I keep putting onions in the guacamole? Is that what you're really saying?"

"You believe I hate your family because I want to stay home on Thanksgiving? Did I understand you correctly?"

Remember, your goal is to pinpoint the connectors that their thought process hinges upon. Therefore your tone needs to be as neutral as possible. If you sound accusatory, they will shut down immediately. Your tone, facial expression and message should be in perfect alignment.

Paraphrasing also lets the other person hear their message played back to them, and gives them a chance to moderate their response—and that's always a good thing, because it means tempers are coming down.

Singing the praise of the paraphrase

In our Verbal Defense & Influence workbook we list a number of benefits that paraphrasing brings to you in the midst of conflict. Here are some of them:

- You can interrupt someone and not generate resistance.
  Nothing calms down an angry person like saying, *"Hold on, let me make sure I understand..."*
- If you've misunderstood, you can be corrected and get it right.
- It creates empathy—the other person will believe you are trying to understand.
- It often makes the other person modify his or her initial statements because they get to hear their meaning in different words and tones.

Lesson 16: Summarize and move ahead

Once you're clear on the message, you comprehend the situation and can move toward resolution. The final stage of the listening process is to recap what you both know, and verbalize where you're going.

Remember, the purpose of Beyond Active Listening is goal-driven, and therefore moving forward with compliance / cooperation collaboration depends on taking action.

This final step is crucial: without it you're exiting the scene with unfinished business. Imagine a parent holding a difficult, my-child-is-bullied conversation with a teacher. Unless that parent walks away with a plan of action (or at least some agreement on next steps), that meeting was well-intentioned but ineffective. Summarizing provides a much stronger point for departure.

"Now that you have some idea what Jimmy has been experiencing, you said you'll move his desk and keep an eye on the situation. Could we connect again in a week to compare notes and be sure things are improving?"

As the Beyond Active Listening process concludes, everyone should walk away from the conversation with a clear understanding and movement toward progress.

Hmm...am I listening?

It takes real work to engage in Beyond Active Listening. Here are some questions to stay keyed in:

WHO am I dealing with? Listen with proper alertness and you'll determine what type of person you are dealing with. Sure, you'll encounter some people who will give you pushback—but your guidance and empathy (and the use of asking, paraphrasing and summarizing) will unlock their resistance.

WHAT are they trying to tell me? Step back and look at the bigger picture: what's the full story? There's more than one side to a story.

When someone is telling you their point of view, they're relating it through their own lens (especially if they're under stress).

That is going to color the story. Make sure to consider:

- Situation and context: For instance, a child who is tired from last night's sleepover might just be upset when he says, *"Mom! I hate you!"* To empathize, you can ask for clarification: *"What happened that made you upset?"*
- Unmet needs: If you are engaging in Beyond Active Listening and encountering resistance, they might not be doing so just to be stubborn. Perhaps their physical needs (sleep nourishment, warmth, or a bathroom break) are overriding their ability to reason.
- Nonverbal cues: Watch for disconnect between what someone is saying and what he or she is doing. You can say, *"I'm not angry,"* but if you continue to clench your teeth and flex your fists I'm not buying it.

Always remember that the message is more than another person's words—and that there's an art to reading between the lines.

"Listening to the message is important, but it's just as important to pick up what's not being said," said Verbal Defense & Influence Director Gary T. Klugiewicz.

WHEN will this make sense to me?

- Have they made their point yet? Some people beat around the bush and take forever to say what they mean. You need to pinpoint the gist of their message, and respond to that and not the peripherals.

- Have I accurately deciphered the message? Paraphrase it back to them until you have comprehended exactly what they mean.

WHERE is this person emotionally? My daughter's personality can split right in half. With her, I have the luxury of knowing whether I'm facing Glenda the Good or the Elphaba the Wicked because she gets so visibly emotional.

I don't have that ability with acquaintances or strangers, but I do know how anger, rage, fear and vulnerability can negatively effect a person's otherwise good nature.

Listen for emotional indicators such as the pitch, speed and tone of their voice. And watch for eye contact, body posture and other nonverbals.

Regardless of whether you are dealing with someone you know or not, your ability to get things done depends upon your ability to cut across the differences and connect—unless, of course, you're not even listening.

CHAPTER 6 CHALLENGE

Turn to the Communicating Under Pressure chart (page 12) and to see how the Beyond Active Listening skills covered in Chapter Six fit in.

1. Briefly elaborate the reasons for engaging in Beyond Active Listening:
   - Compliance
   - Cooperation
   - Collaboration

2. Think of some personal examples of listening with all your senses, not just your ears (don't forget to include your sixth sense, intuition).

3. Consider this statement: Beyond Active Listening is a process in which you work to direct their desires to align with your intentions. What does this mean to you?

4. How can you apply these techniques of Beyond Active Listening?
   - Empathize: Try to imagine what the other person is experiencing
   - Ask to clarify: Using questions to help understand their viewpoint
   - Restating the problem: Using your words to reframe the issue
   - Summarizing and moving ahead: Not wrapping things up until you've planned out your further course of action.

Chapter 7

In the moment:

How to respond to pushback and verbal resistance

Overview: When you encounter negativity, you need to know how to steer clear of conflict and bring resolution by using strategies to redirect, persuade and take action.

All of the strategies we've learned so far have been getting us ready for the moment of encounter:

- Your outlook supports dignity and respect (Five Maxims).
- You appear professional and confident (Showtime).
- You know what to say (Universal Greeting).
- You understand the situation and the viewpoint of the other person (Beyond Active Listening).

For many situations in everyday life, these tactics suffice to prevent and defuse the little dust-ups that come your way. But not always.

At some point, you are going to hit the brick wall, where another person digs in. They might get verbally abusive, or they might say no to your request—or both. Consider how these situations could get negative:

- *"Can you turn the music down?"*
- *"Could you stop hitting my car with the soccer ball?"*
- *"Can you make your dog stop barking all night?"*
- *"Could you not curse during our meetings?"*

At this point, cooperation, collaboration or simple compliance may seem like unattainable goals.

We are now at the heat of the moment and need responsive strategies to help us choreograph this interaction peaceably, in the face of resistance, harassment or negativity.

The techniques we will be learning in this chapter—Redirections and the Persuasion Sequence—will be the basic go-to tools in your toolkit. First, we'll cover the Redirections, which are the tools you need for responding to verbal abuse. Then, we'll move into the Persuasion Sequence, which offers a response when someone refuses to work with you and comply with your requests.

They are tools—not just theory. When you're at this point of conflict you need a solid structure around your words-to-action sequence, so your response becomes practiced and repeatable.

This consistency has critical value for anyone who manages people; you are establishing a track record of observable and predictable decisiveness. These tactics address how to deflect negativity and bring about the desired behavior.

You will know the formula for determining if your verbal requests have failed—and when to take further action.

Repetitive use of these strategies for redirecting and persuading is key to Danielle Shryock's ability to manage her middle school science classroom.

Students, when faced with a consistent response over and over from their teacher, soon realize that they can't push her buttons. They understand the ground rules and before long, they are parroting her responses (the very same tactics that you will be learning here) and using them to address interactions on their own.

"Pretty soon the students are managing themselves and we have achieved a self-policing classroom," Shryock said.

Lesson 17: Understanding resistance

If you tell someone something they don't want to hear, you can't be surprised if you get a little pushback. It often comes in the following forms:

- *Why not?*
- *Who are you to tell me no?*
- *What gives you the right?*
- *What's in it for me?*

It should come as no surprise that you hear those words when you tell someone no. Because face it, you'd ask the same thing.

These are reasonable questions, especially in a country like mine, where we cherish personal freedom and question authority. We call them the Great American Questions.

This shouldn't be considered resistance—yet.

Once you start using a Universal Greeting, one that clearly identifies you, your authority and your purpose, you'll soon discover that the Universal Greeting circumvents these questions because you've already addressed many of their concerns.

If you've gone Beyond Active Listening and are still getting flack, the Persuasion Sequence covered in this chapter will let you address higher levels of resistance.

But really, fundamentally you need to recognize the difference between legitimate questions and active resistance, and then respond with the appropriate level of persuasion.

You'll find yourself taking mild resistance in stride because you understand when to be concerned, or when to let it ride.

Lesson 18: How to handle an insult

Back in Chapter 1 we covered the need for a heightened sense of alertness that keeps you tuned into potential conflict. We called it the "punch you should have heard coming."

Think of insults and verbal resistance like a verbal smack to the head.

You should handle these "punches" verbally the same way you would handle them physically: Block and redirect.

For a physical punch you'd hold up your hand, brush away the strike and step aside. You can do the same thing with your words.

Now it's time to learn how to redirect. The act of Redirection is a two-step process of deflecting the insult and redirecting their focus.

To deflect the insult, use a short phrase that enables you to dodge a verbal attack. Deliver it reflexively, immediately and without a trace of emotion:

>*"Whoa, I get that you're angry, I'd be angry too…"*
>
>*"I'm hearing you, but we've got to deal with this…"*
>
>*"I get your point and I see where you're coming from but…"*

This enables you to essentially step aside and move on. Now it's time to redirect the other person's behavior or emotion.

Redirections fall into categories: serious, funny, apologetic or polite threats. There's a wide variety of responses based on the situation and your own personality—for example, some might be comfortable using humor, while others want to focus on the facts of the situation.

Here's the two-part sequence: deflect the verbal assault, then redirect them back to your goal by using professional language. For example:

- *"Is there something I did to make you angry at me? I apologize if I did something wrong. But I'm going to ask you not to treat me that way."* (apologetic)
- *"I understand that you're upset but may I ask that you not call me a name like that?"* (serious)
- *"I know you're a reasonable person; let's figure this out together and let's not have to get Dad involved."* (polite threat)

Because the insults can trigger us from deep within, our response must be preplanned and practiced. Our trainers, for example, build a great deal of small group and partner drills to make sure students are comfortable performing Redirections. You can't just know them—in the heat of the moment you need to deliver a home run, and that kind of performance only comes with practice.

It's important to end your deflection on a positive note. Always follow up a deflection with a message that focuses on the resolution of the issue:

>*"I understand that you're angry and I appreciate your viewpoint—but this is about finding a way to not argue every time we see one another. I would like*

for us to get along."

Now, keep in mind that the purpose of Redirections is not to shut down the person altogether. They might be justifiably angry. From the standpoint of empathy, you need to get a sense of where they're coming from.

Instead of using this technique to simply power forward, you might opt to step back and take a moment to engage in the steps of Beyond Active Listening from the previous chapter:

- Listen with all your senses
- Empathize
- Ask for clarification
- Paraphrase
- Summarize

Yes, your goal is to move past the insult—but make sure you are duly listening and not just sailing through. Acting dismissively would violate our fundamental approach of treating people with dignity by showing them respect.

What to do when they say no

The Persuasion Sequence kicks in when you need someone to modify their behavior. It's a scripted approach to get someone else to stop doing wrong and start doing right.

The Persuasion Sequence is one of the more well-known tenets of Verbal Defense & Influence. Just as the Universal Greeting is a scripted approach to making initial contact, the Persuasion Sequence takes you step-by-step through the process of gaining compliance, cooperation, and collaboration.

As you work through the sequence you will realize that none of these concepts are new to you—they're embedded in the Universal Greeting, the Five Maxims, Beyond Active Listening and more.

These concepts are not just theory. They don't just lay the groundwork. They are actionable even at the point of impact.

"Our philosophy is also our tactic," said Verbal Defense & Influence

Director Gary T. Klugiewicz.

Words, ideas and actions—they must come together in perfect alignment. Nothing demonstrates your personal integrity better than by saying what you mean and acting upon what you say.

Lesson 19: The Persuasion Sequence

The Persuasion Sequence is effective regardless of the scale of the interaction. Let's start with a minor scenario that some of us would struggle with: making initial contact with a stranger at the movie theater and assertively asking them to turn off their phone.

1. **Ask, don't tell**

   "Now that the movie has started, could you please stop texting?"
   You're requesting, not bossing them around.
   This might be enough to get them to comply. If not, let's move on to Step 2.

2. **Explain why / set context**

   "The light from the phone is distracting those of us around you, so could you please put your phone away?
   Explain the effect that their behavior is having on the situation. By this point most people will comply. If not, it's time to remember it's Showtime: breathe, stack your blocks and gain control of your response so you don't get sucked into acting badly. Once you've gained your emotional equilibrium, move on to Step 3.

3. **Give options, not threats**

   "I know you paid good money to see this, and I want you to see the show."
   (positive option)
   "I don't want to get a manager involved because they'd make you leave and you'd be out cold. (negative option) *"So why not sit back and enjoy?"*

You've politely informed them of your intention to notify the management.

You've also presented them with options by reminding them of the good money they paid to be here. And you've painted a pretty lousy picture of what the rest of their night would be like: out cold.

You don't have to follow a pattern—you might just want to point out the positive options they have before them. If you do give them negative options, be sure to follow up with a positive note at the end. It helps accentuate the positive, and it makes the negative option sound less like a threat.

The power of options

We're going to take a quick pause from progressing through the Persuasion Sequence to emphasize the importance of good options.

In the world of Verbal Defense & Influence, presenting a non-compliant person with solid, appealing options is what makes the world go around.

To understand good options, let's contrast them with some not-so-good options:

- *If you don't pick up your toys, you won't get to bed on time.*
- *Sit down and shut up or get out.*
- *It's my way or the highway.*
- *This is your last chance.*

In the world of persuasion, these options stink. If I were presented with any of them, I'd burst into flames.

Options must empower, build buy-in and promote a change in behavior. They must be the options of the do-er, not the talker.

Getting to bed on time, for example, is a lousy option. It motivates no red-blooded kid on the planet. While having kids in bed is highly motivating to, say, their mother, the mother's behavior is not the issue.

It's tricky to construct motivators that are meaningful to someone else when your own motivators—the promise of a quiet night and a glass of Merlot—are desperately consuming.

You need the empathy to see the situation through their eyes. A quick round of cards or an extra five minutes before bed are much more motivating to a kid.

Remember the words of Kenneth Cook: our challenge is making their desires (not ours) match up with our objectives.

4. Give a second chance

Now let's hop back on the Persuasion Sequence track and talk about how the second chance embraces or declines compliance. Back at the movie theater, the next step in asking a fellow patron to turn off the phone would sound like:

"Is there anything I can say to get you to turn off your phone? I'd like to think so."

You're double-checking their response in hopes of peaceable resolution.

The Persuasion Sequence has, to this point, matched up with the Five Maxims of Human Interaction: Listen. Ask / Don't tell. Explain why. Offer options, not threats. Give a second chance.

This is not a coincidence—it's proof of the remarkable power of cause-and-effect. Having the proper mindset will drive appropriate response.

5. Take appropriate action

Rarely, the Persuasion Sequence gets to the point where words have stopped working. But if it reaches that point, you need to take action.

Set down your popcorn and go talk to the manager. You have reached the point where your words have proven ineffective.

There's nothing more to say.

Lesson 20: Identifying When Words Alone Fail

You've made your way through the entire Persuasion Sequence and they still haven't budged. It's pretty unlikely that they will comply if you keep talking at them.

Yet we do it all the time, repeat ourselves and our directive—put that down, get away, cut it out—despite the fact that we are getting less and less effective with every breath.

Instead of repeating a command over and over and becoming excessively repetitive, the Persuasion Sequence alerts you that you need to reach deeper into your bag of persuasion tools.

You are at the stage When Words Alone Fail. Sometimes this can happen. This failure of the Persuasion Sequence can be due to a number of reasons:

1. You've tried the Persuasion Sequence and it didn't work.
2. The Persuasion Sequence isn't appropriate or it's simply inadequate for the circumstances.
3. There might be an imminent safety threat to someone (they're coming at you, they're going to hurt themselves, they're in the act of damaging your property, etc.) that requires you to take immediate action.

Let's take the comment from a few pages back: *"Can you make your dog stop barking all night?"* Let's say the neighbor is resistant at every point and you need to follow the entire Persuasion Sequence:

Ask, don't tell: *"Can you get your dog to stop barking all night?"*

Neighbor: No.

Explain why: *"My daughter is having a hard time falling asleep. Could you help her sleep by getting your dog to be quieter?"*

Neighbor: Nope.

Give options, not threats: *"I appreciate that your dog is part of your family, but his barking violates our community's noise ordinance. I don't want to see you getting a citation"* (polite threat).

Neighbor: Forget it.

Give a second chance: *"Is there anything I can say to get you to work with me on keeping the noise down?"*

Neighbor: No way.

Take appropriate action: Disengage from the conversation and consider your options.

What action you take and how you take it is determined by where this situation falls along the spectrum of danger or violence.

Recall Chapter 2, when we discussed how to read a situation and develop an appropriate response.

You should have a sense of your viable and realistic options because you have been engaged in when-then thinking and have been assessing the situation as it notches up in intensity.

Having reached the end of the Persuasion Sequence means that you can consider your neighbor non-compliant. What are your options? You could file a complaint with your neighborhood association or the police or, if this is a consistent problem, talk to an alderman about proposing new dog control legislation.

A better way to say no

We can't always give others—our friends, our family, or the people we serve—what they think they want, for a whole lot of reasons.

It might not be safe, convenient, or permissible. And so our task becomes bringing them down gently and moving on.

When you are placed in the position of telling someone no, you should anticipate pushback and verbal resistance. These tactics address how to deflect the negativity and bring about the desired behavior. By following this formula you'll know if your verbal requests have failed—and when to take further action.

For the security teams, law enforcement officers and corporate risk managers we teach, the revelation comes when they discover that this reframes the very scope and purpose of their jobs.

No longer are they in the business of compliance enforcement—even the rule-wielding baseball umpires see the bigger picture. They come to realize the greater purpose of generating cooperation and protecting others. They become guardians from within.

The transformation is even greater when bullied children and adults tap into their own assertiveness and stop granting their tormentors power over their response. They now have a pathway to gain control and become custodians of their own safety.

Keeping watch

No one likes to be told no. And yet the task falls upon so many of us every single day: Elementary school secretaries, for example, must guard the doors and control access to the building. That's a weighty safety responsibility embedded into an otherwise administrative job.

Potentially resistant encounters like this are all in a day's work for so many professions, not just managers. Do any of these sound familiar to you?

- *I'm sorry, you can't take that bag into the dressing room.*
- *Cell phones may not be used in the hospital.*
- *There are children here; please consider your language.*

Being the hall monitor might not be part of anyone's job description, but it's such a common task nowadays, working in public settings, that our trainers use this as a scenario when they conduct role-play activities of the Universal Greeting (Chapter 6):

- *Hello, my name is Kathy, I work here on the second floor.*
- *The reason I stopped over is that you look new here.*
- *Are you trying to locate an office or person specifically?*
- *May I assist you?*

As you'll see in the next chapter, participating in the wellness and safety of our schools, workplaces and communities improves social conditions—as long as everyone knows how to engage safely.

CHAPTER 7 CHALLENGE

Turn to the Communicating Under Pressure chart (page 12) to see how the following concepts fit in.

- Redirections
- Persuasion Sequence
- When Words Alone Fail

1. Do the four Great American Questions give you a new understanding of mild and severe resistance?
   - Why not?
   - Who are you to tell me no?
   - What gives you the right?
   - What's in it for me?

   Will you adjust your response to pushback based upon this insight?

2. Picture yourself blocking and moving away from a verbal assault much like you'd respond to a physical punch. Does this image of moving aside and deflecting help you understand how to better respond to insults?

3. Recall a verbal insult directed at you. Can you adapt one of our Redirections for that situation?

4. Let's say you need to ask your neighbors to turn the music down. How would you:
   - Ask for clarification?
   - Explain why/set context?
   - Offer options, not threats?
   - Give a second chance?

5. In the example above, what are some of the that indicating that when talking to your neighbor, your words alone have failed?

6. Is it easy for you to tell someone no? How will the techniques in this chapter make the job easier?

Chapter 8

The bigger picture:

How to improve the atmosphere

Overview: So much of the time, the major problems within our environment stem from minor issues that have not been adequately addressed. To counter negativity and conflict within your private sphere, start at the root.

The purpose of building skills for confidence in conflict is actually two-fold. First, it's about building your capacity to defuse and de-escalate situations in which conflict is present.

Second, these skills can help you create non-escalatory environments, that is, places in which conflict is not encouraged.

These techniques should have you feeling both proactive and responsive. You not only have the capability to address conflicts that flare up, you also have the tools to calm down a situation and prevent conflict before it hits the crisis point.

The focus of this chapter is to explain the concept of a social contract, and how these non-escalatory and de-escalatory strategies meld together when creating a peaceable environment.

Earlier in the book I explained that atmospheres can go one of two ways, they can be either emotionally supportive or defensive. Only the supportive environment is compatible with the priority goal of treating people with dignity by showing them respect.

Let's begin our discussion by describing the social contract, then detail how to use a social contract to create and maintain a supportive atmosphere. Finally, we'll show how to create a robust and functional social contract within those places that matter most to you.

What is a social contract?

A social contract is like a playbook that members of a group use to cultivate an environment where everyone:

- Understands the rules,
- Agrees to follow the rules,
- Functions within the rules, and
- Helps maintain the rules.

You'll notice that a social contract is driven by rules, but it is more than the rules alone. We all know of places (schools and workplaces included) that have rules posted on the wall, but which are not followed, enforced or embraced.

A social contract, on the other hand, cultivates buy-in and creates a supportive atmosphere.

In Chapter Four we met Danielle Shryock, a middle school teacher who practices Verbal Defense & Influence in her classroom. Let's walk through her approach at building up a social contract.

Establishing the social contract is a priority from the very first moments of school. She spends the first days of school with her students, pinpointing the needs of the group, working up a set of expectations for the group and building buy-in.

By the end of that initial process, the group has jointly determined the type of learning atmosphere they expect, and have had a hand in shaping the rules. They have a vision for the classroom they want. It's not about Shryock's expectations anymore.

"We create an agreement on how we're going to treat each other," she said.

But it doesn't stop there. Using strategies like the Universal Greeting, Redirections and the Persuasion Sequence, she upholds the social contract with consistent techniques for managing disruptions.

It doesn't take long before students know what kind of consequences to expect, as well as how those expectations would be enforced.

"I use the same phrases consistently to redirect and counter verbal resistance," she said. "I start to hear them parroting my language."

Pretty soon, the students were using these techniques on their own, with one another.

They internalize the language of expectations and consequences. Shryock had achieved her goal of what she calls a "self-policing classroom."

"They learn to manage each other."

Shryock's "self-policing classroom" is an excellent example of a social contract that functions as a framework for behavior. Everyone knows the rules, as well as what to say to make sure the group's behavior falls within its parameters.

Schools and classroom environments that don't have this self-policing quality suffer from a broken social contract—the rules may indeed be present, but they are not being enforced or upheld by all the members of the community.

A place where everyone knows the rules

Places in which rules are internalized and implicitly followed might seem like exotic and faraway lands. But they exist all around us. You just need to know what you're looking for.

Joel Lashley, one of our most in-demand consultants particularly within hospitals and health care, described the atmosphere at a place that many of us have visited: the public library.

"Everyone—no matter who they are—knows to keep quiet at a library. If I decide to make noise, members of the group (not just the librarians) will look at me disapprovingly," he said. "If I'm still noisy the librarian might come over and shush me. If I'm still loud I can get kicked out—just because I'm making a little noise."

Everyone knows what's expected at the library, and everyone from the staff to the patrons uphold those expectations. Now that's a functional social contract.

High standards, low threshold

How do you create an atmosphere that is incompatible with undesirable behavior?

Lashley, who is also the security training director at a major children's hospital, trains extensively within hospital and health care settings (environments where the workers are five times more likely to be assaulted at work than the general population). He explained that setting out to create non-escalatory environments is a work-in-constant progress, one that requires constant maintenance.

Creating a non-escalatory environment involves lowering the threshold of tolerance, Lashley said, nipping minor issues in the bud and preventing them from growing into larger problems.

In order for that to take place, however, we first need to acknowledge that even low-level behaviors can escalate upwards on the spectrum of violence.

Lowering our threshold of tolerance

At what point does violence begin? Is it physical force? Angry words? Malicious intent?

Hospitals, for example, experience high levels of workplace violence. Nurses are shoved, pushed and punched on a regular basis. But instead of honing in and focusing upon the physical acts of assault, Lashley taught hospital staff to be vigilant against the presence of what he calls "gateway behaviors."

Gateway behaviors are acts that foreshadow worse acts of disrespect—including physical violence—to come. Lashley has found that if low-level infractions such as swearing, demeaning language and yelling, are discouraged, the environment becomes less vulnerable to grievous offenses.

Lesson 21: Recognize and address gateway behaviors

When a gateway behavior is ignored it is implicitly being tolerated, Lashley said. And that makes it a springboard into progressively worse behavior.

He draws a parallel between gateway behaviors and the concept of gateway drugs—once you've gotten accustomed to "starter" drugs, you find more potent drugs alluring, and your problems escalate exponentially.

At Lashley's hospital, they found that drawing the line on swearing led to a more peaceable atmosphere. And the tools they use to draw the line are the Verbal Defense & Influence tactics you've already learned.

Every person within the emergency room, from the receptionist to the triage nurse, has learned and practiced the hospital's scripted response. When they encounter a patient who is swearing they can immediately address the problem. Notice how they apply a Universal Greeting that seamlessly integrates with the Persuasion Sequence:

Universal Greeting: *"Excuse me, my name is Joel and I am a security manager at the hospital. The reason I'm here is to talk to you about acceptable language here."*

Persuasion Sequence: *"Could I ask you to stop using that kind of language here in a children's hospital?*

"It upsets the children around us.

"Could I ask you to please consider these children and use appropriate language here in the waiting room?"

You'll note that this is a masterful application of Verbal Defense & Influence tenets: asking instead of telling them to stop, explaining why, and above all, treating them with dignity by showing respect.

By eliminating gateway behaviors, that hospital staff is effectively creating a social contract for acceptable conduct.

Once members of the group understand and act upon the need to stop swearing (i.e. maintaining a healing environment for kids), they are implicitly agreeing to hold themselves to higher standards.

If they agree not to swear, they probably won't push, shove or punch. The would-be violator hasn't just stopped a negative behavior; they've bought into the social contract.

LESSON 22: Applying these lessons at home

We've mentioned the concept of a social contract at various points throughout the chapter; it's worthwhile to recap once again. A place with a robust social contract has universal buy-in. It is a place where everyone:

- Understands the rules,
- Agrees to follow the rules,
- Functions within the rules and
- Helps maintain the rules.

Does this sound like the setup in your home? Yeah, it's not always so utopian in mine, either.

In order for this structure to work, there needs to be consistency, or the littlest things can tip the scales. Typically they're easy to identify in retrospect.

But looking back lets us review and make changes for the better (we get deep into that idea in Chapter 10). So let me tell you a simple story about a minor irritation that I mistakenly let slide.

From cookie to feeding frenzy

Few things are as relentless as an 11-year-old with a sweet tooth.

"Can I have two cookies? What about a cookie and four jellybeans? What about eight jellybeans instead?" My daughter just keeps chipping away at my resolve to not let her snack on junk food.

Yes, there have been times that I've caved in just to make my daughter go away. In fact, she is so good that her older brothers send her to do the negotiating; when she's badgered me to the breaking point they swoop in and collect the goodies.

The next thing I'd know all three of them are ravaging the kitchen looking for more snacks. What started as a few cookies has turned into a three-shark feeding frenzy.

It's affected my dinner plans—no one is hungry anymore—and has left my kitchen a mess.

In retrospect it's so easy to identify the point at which I could have addressed the gateway behavior. It would have put an end to the nonsense and steered things in a different direction.

I appreciate the fact that you're hungry (empathize), so why don't you have an apple? (redirect).

The cookies are for dessert (tell them why).

In fact, why don't you choose whether you want an apple or some pretzels (offer options, not threats)?

If I don't address her wheedling consistently, you can be sure that she'll be asking the same question the next day and the next. The answer needs to be clear and consistent; there can be no chinks in my armor.

The bigger point

When my daughter wins this battle, there's quite a bit at stake. It's not just about the cookies—it's about our household expectations. Asserting her influence has eroded our accepted system.

There are bigger issues embedded in such seemingly mundane interactions, and that's why they deserve attention.

If she wins at cookies today, she'll want to ratchet up the power game and challenge even more of our house rules.

A final word about those cookies

In this chapter we've caught glimpses of what gateway behaviors can look like at home and at work.

The common theme to healthy environments is the strength and durability of the social contract. That is a message to take to heart.

The Five Maxims have served that purpose, offering a solid platform for being both flexible and firm. It offers a blueprint for holding up a robust social contract in the face of resistance.

My family has learned that by operating under a consistent structure, they will always receive respect in a supportive atmosphere.

They won't get that cookie before dinner. But they'll always receive a huge helping of respect (even between meals).

CHAPTER 8 CHALLENGE

Using what you've learned about social contracts, consider these questions. Turn to the Communicating Under Pressure chart (page 12) for review.

1. Consider the communities that you participate in—home, school, church, social groups, teams, workplace, etc. How strong are the social contracts based upon these criteria?
    - Everyone understands the rules.
    - Everyone agrees to follow the rules.
    - Everyone functions within the rules.
    - Everyone helps maintain the rules.

2. Have you ever been in an environment like the "self-policing" classroom mentioned in this chapter?

    How were the rules internalized and enforced?

3. Think about the communities you listed in Question 1.

    What are gateway behaviors that lead to bigger problems?

    Do you have ideas on how to address these gateway behaviors before they lead to bigger problems?

Chapter 9

Step up:

How to engage bystanders

Overview: Upholding a social contract can be a group effort, as long as everyone in the group (including bystanders) knows how to intervene and protect.

Harassment, emotional abuse and verbal violence don't take place within a vacuum. There are usually bystanders, quasi-participants who bear witness.

This chapter is about empowering the bystanders to take action. It is a promising new area of focus for those of us who train others to become more confident in conflict.

To state it simply, bystanders rarely intervene, because they don't know how or if they should. But when they do step in, this peer-to-peer intervention is highly effective at putting an end to conflict.

A number of years ago Verbal Defense & Influence Director Gary T. Klugiewicz wrote an article called "The Bully Cycle," in which he listed the parties involved in bullying:

- The targeted child,
- The bully, and
- The larger group that allows the bullying to accur.

The larger group is made up of both peer group members and persons in authority who allow bullying to occur and continue.

"A key point is that bullying continues in any setting only when the group permits it through a sick sort of co-dependency," he wrote. "Bullying occurs because we—the bully, the bullied, the peer group and the persons in authority—allow it.

"Who is responsible for keeping members of our school, group or workplace safe? We all are."

When conflict is taking place, it's Showtime for bystanders, too.

To intervene requires situational awareness, empathy and skills for communicating under pressure.

This chapter details the journey of how mindsets shift, skills increase, confidence grows and bystanders become protectors.

Harnessing the collective power

Statistics reveal that people who are bystanders have the power to turn negative situations around an astonishing 85 percent of the time—when they intervene and get involved.

The sad reality however is that studies have shown bystanders intervene only 11 percent of the time.

How do we increase the capacity for bystanders to step up and try to do the right thing? Interestingly, colleges and universities have been at the forefront of both bystander intervention research and campus programming.

Colleges and universities have long struggled with the negative consequences of what can happen when young people come together in community, particularly when it comes to sexual violence. Because of the great risk to their institutions, universities have been at the forefront of developing bystander intervention initiatives.

Vistelar consultant Jill Weisensel, one of the co-developers of Marquette University's bystander training, said these bystander-based solutions have widespread applicability well beyond the college setting:

Other kids can stop bullying on the playground. Co-workers can shut down toxic behavior in the workplace.

Here's what this means to people who aren't directly part of the problem: You can make a difference.

Is this my problem?

Let's say you're in a group and someone is starting to insult another person. What do you do?

1. Keep quiet and not draw attention—after all, it's not your problem.
2. Act distracted and pretend you aren't listening.
3. Tell them it's making you uncomfortable.
4. You were texting your girlfriend and never even noticed.

Wouldn't we love to answer #3, and be one of those people who can speak for the silent majority, who want an unpleasant situation to end?

But social inertia is difficult to overcome, and realistically most of us silently bide our time until the discomfort has passed.

We probably fall into categories 1 or 2, and are prone to disengage. Few of us possess the silver-tongued ability to know the words that will extinguish the conversation without turning the flames back on us. In the absence of intervention skills (and the confidence they bring), we do and say nothing. And by distancing ourselves we disclaim responsibility and absolve ourselves from culpability.

Or, we fall into category #4 and never even notice that there is a problem developing right before our eyes. As you recall from the last chapter on social contracts, large-scale problems can be dramatically reduced when we step in and address low-level gateway behaviors. But when we're so preoccupied and plugged into our cell phones, we aren't paying attention until things get out of control.

Being aware of your surroundings and your circumstances will bring about the realization that on some level, you have a measure of responsibility over the words, ideas and behaviors happening within your space.

Lesson 23: Observe and evaluate

Being aware of the social dynamics within the group will only build the bridge halfway. Bystanders must also interpret the situation as a problem and assess the risks; otherwise, they will see no need to intervene.

- Michael might normally be able to tolerate some ribbing on the playground about being short. But maybe today Michael feels emotionally vulnerable, or the insults have gotten out of hand. Unless someone perceives this change in the atmosphere and recognizes its overtones, whether it's in the tone of the insults or in Michael's reaction, the situation will escalate.
- Sarah is at the college bar with her friends. She has been drinking; now she is flirting with a stranger and it is beginning to get out of control. Unless her friends notice the problem, consider the possible outcome and guide her away, she may find herself in a compromised situation.
- A conversation among a group of friends has turned inappropriate. Unless someone senses the downturn, recognizes the risk of offending members of the group and steers it back on track, the language and the content of the conversation will get offensive.

The ability to interpret an event as a potential problem involves developing both empathy and the ability to forecast the rest of the story:

1. How would I feel if this was happening to me?
2. Where could this end up if I don't say or do something?

Bystanders and the social contract

Recall that when we discussed supportive environments in the last chapter, we pointed out that upholding this environment takes work, and that the work falls on the group in its entirety, not just those in authority.

For example, the teacher with her "self-policing classroom" relies on all the students to intervene and correct when they see something going wrong.

The checks and balances don't come from the top-down; in an optimal environment it's up to everyone to enforce the expectations.

If there's already a social contract established, in which everyone understands and follows the rules, it's much easier to have a conversation about living up to expectations. This holds true whether the environment happens to be a team locker room or your own dinner table.

Lesson 24: Intervene appropriately

If you notice a problem, you need to know the appropriate tactics for resolving the situation.

It's too bad that the concept of intervention conjures some scary mental images, like untying a maiden from the train tracks or rushing into a burning building to save a baby. These intimidating associations prevent many of us bystanders from fully engaging.

There are low-level intervention options, however, that don't involve getting in the middle of fights or putting yourself in a threatening position—and they are highly effective.

The University of Arizona's STEP UP program, for example, stresses the need for bystanders to develop engagement skills—such as the Verbal Defense & Influence concepts within this book.

Remember, the Persuasion Sequence is the primary tool in your toolkit for stopping inappropriate behavior, so give it a try: *"Could you please stop teasing Michael? It looks like he's no longer having fun."* Or, *"Sarah, why don't you come hang out with all of us?"*

It doesn't matter if the bad behavior is happening to you, or whether you are witnessing it happening to another member of your group. The structure of the Persuasion Sequence remains constant. The rules of delivering this type of message are consistent as well.

"The person intervening should conduct the conversation in a safe environment, while being conscious of delivery style (tone, word choice and the other non-verbals) necessary to convey a sensitive, understanding, non-judgmental, and empathetic approach," said Weisensel.

It takes good judgment and solid skills to know when, where, why and how to tell someone their actions or words are inappropriate. When these programs are delivered at her university, for example, they are done by peer leaders trained by Weisensel to conduct role-play scenarios and lead discussions about possible strategies for bystander intervention in college settings:

- Remind a friend that he or she could lose their athletic scholarship.
- Pull out your cell phone at the bar and offer to take a picture of

your friend and the stranger who is hitting on her (perpetrators will run at the first sight of a camera).

- Make a manager aware of a problem at their restaurant or store, so they can address it appropriately.
- Designate a non-drinker within a group of friends who ensures everyone gets safely home.

The more targeted these scenarios are to the setting the better—obviously the examples for a high school or workplace would reflect the issues and settings for bystanders in those environments.

LESSON 25: Speak up

Weisensel also recommended having a number of what she calls "Engagement Phrases" at the ready, to shut down negative gateway behaviors and conversations before they escalate.

Think about it—you're delivering Verbal Defense & Influence Redirections from the sidelines:

- *"I know you are better than that."*
- *"You know that's not OK."*
- *"I hope no one talks about you like that."*
- *"Wow, do you really feel that way about "x" person/group/behavior."*
- *"I didn't expect that from you."*
- *"Could you please choose another word?"*
- Addressing the group: *"Was that as wrong to you as it was to me?"*

Engaged peers who are committed to upholding the social climate can motivate and inspire change—as long as members can define what behavior will and won't be tolerated.

Treat people with dignity by showing them respect. That's the foundation of the Five Maxims in the midst of conflict, even if we're "just" standing by.

Protectors notice. Protectors engage.

It's time to stop ignoring the plight of others, or willfully overlooking words and behavior that fall into the grey zone of inappropriateness.

Fortunately, protectors like you can bring the language of peace.

CHAPTER 9 CHALLENGE

Using what you've learned about bystander dynamics, consider these questions. Turn to the Communicating Under Pressure chart (page 12) and see how Bystander Mobilization fits in.

1. The concept of bystander intervention doesn't play out exclusively on college campuses or schoolyard playgrounds. Consider how group dynamics function within your personal and professional groups. Who are the bystanders? Would they be influential in addressing negativity?

2. How could Confidence in Conflict help bystanders in your environment develop:
   - Situational awareness
   - Empathy
   - Skills for communicating under pressure

3. Brainstorm some ways that bystanders could use Beyond Active Listening skills to:
   - Notice the problem and assume responsibility.
   - Interpret the problem and assess risk.

4. How could bystanders use a Universal Greeting, Redirections and the Persuasion Sequence to:
   - Engage effectively and safely?
   - Manage verbal resistance?

5. Which Engagement Phrases would work best within your groups?

Chapter 10

Moving ahead:

How to improve future behavior

Overview: Achieving confidence in conflict isn't just one-and-done. This is a constant process of engagement, review and readjustment. Continue to train and keep improving.

What's the first thing that a football team does the Monday after the game? They get everyone in a room to watch the game and dissect what happened, regardless of whether they won or lost.

Their purpose is not to lay blame or pat one another on the back. That's already taken place. Once the dust has cleared the team's objective is to regroup and move forward.

In Monday's clear light they assess: How can we apply the actions of the past to improve this week's game?

Improving future performance—even in everyday situations—is the direction of this chapter and beyond.

So how did it go?

In order to become proficient, you need more than a set of skills. You need to put in time and effort to operate at peak performance.

It also holds true for maintaining confidence in conflict.

After handling a tense situation, most of us will take a pause, long enough to think, *"Hmm…that went well (or not),"* and then we dive back into our regularly scheduled activities.

We've acknowledged the moment but only in the most superficial sense. We might give it a second thought as we close our eyes before falling asleep, but that's not going to be very constructive—in fact, it will cause us to lose sleep if it didn't go very well.

What we need is a process for reviewing how we performed in the midst of stress for the purpose of building proficiency.

An honest self-assessment is the place to start. And keep in mind that honest doesn't mean dwelling on all the things you did wrong. Later in this chapter we'll cover how important it is to celebrate our "Peace Stories," and value what's gone well.

And finally—particularly when it comes to conflict within our personal circle—we need to reach out and reconnect with the other person, to close out the interaction with as much dignity intact as possible.

For some professionals a review process is built into their procedures. If you don't have a framework for debriefing already, here are some questions that you can use to start the process:

- Is everyone OK?
- What did we do well?
- What have you learned?
- What would you do differently next time?

Moving past the language of blame

Be mindful of how you navigate the situation—the goal of improving future performance is your North Star. The framework you set up for discussions like this will impact the tone of your review. That's why it is so important to take the focus away from what went wrong. Instead, focus on moving ahead.

- If you refer to it strictly as past occurrence, the focus will revolve around laying blame *("here's what happened")*.
- Instead, when you frame it within present tense, you are setting a tone of agreement *("here's what happens when X takes place")*.

- And better still, when you focus on future outcomes you set the tone for the promise of a future payoff or benefit *("Y is possible when X takes place")*.

Instead of creating a defensive atmosphere—one centered on ego, blame and acquittal—the focus should be on identifying chronic patterns of behavior or ongoing situations that need resolution. Think about how you want the situation to go if it were to happen again next week.

And now that you have a framework and a vocabulary to let you pinpoint the skills you need for communicating under pressure, the review process will reveal the skills that need strengthening.

Blame won't make you better. However, staying focused on the future will make you excellent.

Shifting the focus from bad to good

We've all told our share of war stories, those times that we survived the worst of conditions on wits alone.

Yet for some reason we fail to acknowledge the times when things go right.

The theme of the war story is the triumph of self when all else fails. Now I'd like to introduce you to the concept of a "Peace Story," where we attain our triumphs not through chance, but through skill.

We build our interactions with others around the expectation of success. So, if we do a really great job of handling a situation, we aren't likely to give ourselves the proper credit that we deserve.

That lack of credit is both internal—we don't adequately acknowledge a job well done—and it's external too. We don't want to brag or even worse, we truly don't recognize the accomplishment of steering our boat through choppy waters and not capsizing.

How different things would be if we celebrated—or at least noted—the heavy lifting involved in creating peace instead of taking these unsung victories for granted.

For many years Gary T. Klugiewicz has been a head cheerleader of sorts, videotaping and collecting stories of successful communication in action. In fact, it's a requirement for all new Verbal Defense & Influence instructors to reflect upon their experiences and create Peace Stories of their own.

Peace Stories are personal accounts of a situation—similar in format (but not content) to the war stories we've been swapping up until now.

These videos are powerful, because they show confidence in conflict in action. They're not professionally produced, with actors or made-up situations. They're raw, and they're authentic. This growing collection (hundreds upon hundreds of videos so far) represents real-life, real-world effectiveness. It is proof that peace is possible.

Compile a mental list of Peace Stories of your own—they'll serve as a template for future success.

What's next: active engagement

What happens to muscles that aren't being used? They become a flabby mess, of course. That's something you don't want happening to the conflict resolution skills you have been learning.

Early in the book I made a comparison between the Communicating Under Pressure chart and a recipe card for my favorite apple cake.

When I'm in my kitchen the only way to replicate success is to pull out the recipe, use the proper ingredients and follow the directions. Same thing goes for having confidence in conflict. The boilerplate skills and tactics can be used again and again.

Our instructors, advisors and consultants teach these skills in all parts of the country, particularly within workplace environments and schools.

Some levels of training are quite intense—instructors who are certified to teach within their agency undergo a 35-hour block of training. Once certified they need to take occasional refresher courses and re-certify every few years.

Even individuals who take part in shorter seminars, workshops and online classes receive resources designed to keep the material fresh, relevant and inspiring. There are webinars and coaching calls. We even have an annual conference, Beyond Conflict, which has outgrown its venue time and time again.

But when you are really keyed into this material, you don't have to travel places or go online to seek inspiration. It's all around you, once you know how to recognize it.

Being able to manage your emotions and the image you project is fundamental to your ability to respond and not react in the midst of stress. And when conflict does happen, you have the tools to handle stressful situations without losing your cool.

If you're like most people who learn this methodology, this has sparked a major process of personal discovery.

You can respond professionally, even when it's to your 4-year-old child or your 40-year-old brother.

As you've made your way through these chapters you've undoubtedly gone about your interactions with a heightened sense of awareness. You've witnessed blowups at the grocery store and family strife with fresh eyes.

And you have a newfound appreciation for the act of peacemaking, and the even more difficult act of peacekeeping.

You've watched everyday people perform confidently in conflict, affirming the dignity of others using the Five Maxims, displaying their Showtime presence, while at the same time getting results.

You've seen the pros for what they are, and you recognize what your future can hold.

You have become the face of confidence in conflict.

CHAPTER 10 CHALLENGE

1. Have you ever conducted an after-the-fact review of your conflict performance?
2. During a debrief, how can you make sure to focus on future improvement instead of laying blame for past mistakes?
3. Recall 2-3 Peace Stories that you have participated in or witnessed during the course of reading this book.
4. Have you observed someone function well under pressure? Name a person you admire for their conflict resolution abilities.
5. How important is it for you to maintain your conflict resolution "muscles?" Have you subscribed to the blog at www.ConfidenceinConflict.com yet?

REQUEST FOR REVIEWS

Thank you for reading my book! PLEASE REVIEW this book on Amazon. I need your feedback to make the next version better. Thank you so much!

SEND US YOUR PEACE STORY

Now that you've got the techniques and the vocabulary for communicating your skills, please send in a personal story of when you were able to remain effective in the face of conflict. There are regular prizes and giveaways for the best videos and written submissions.

Could you send one in today? Much appreciated!

www.Vistelar.com/PeaceStories

Coming soon: Peace Story companion books for the Confidence in Conflict series. Subscribe to the blog at www.ConfidenceinConflict.com/blog for info on the latest new releases.

About the Author

Kathy Mangold is an award-winning communicator who is committed to conflict resolution strategies built upon a foundation of dignity and respect, even in the midst of stress.

As consultant with the Vistelar Group, Kathy has created educational materials and programming that support Vistelar's Verbal Defense & Influence methodology, which has been taught mainly in professional settings for 30 years.

Her most recent project, Confidence in Conflict for Everyday Life, illustrates how these concepts can be applied within one's personal life. For this project Kathy has drawn from her real-life experiences as the editor of a parenting magazine.

The Vistelar Group is a global training and speaking organization committed to addressing the spectrum of human conflict. Corporate and civic clients include the U.S. Department of Agriculture, Nissan USA, the Mall of America, and police agencies across the country, including Albuquerque, NM and Kalamazoo, MI.

Contact Kathy at Trainers@Vistelar.com.

LESSON REVIEW

Here is collection of the key confidence-building concepts from every chapter. Use this space to write down one or two ideas that will be helpful in applying these ideas to your everyday life.

LESSON 1: Think when, not if

Acknowledging the probability of conflict lessens the potential for disruption when it actually occurs.

_____

_____

_____

LESSON 2: Guard against anger and emotion

Having mental control over your feelings protects you from any type of emotional excess. Emotional reaction should not override your reasoned, rational response.

_____

_____

_____

LESSON 3: Own your triggers

Listing and categorizing your triggers give you the opportunity to anticipate insults and situations that would have otherwise caught you off-guard.

_____

_____

_____

LESSON 4: Adopt tactical thinking

Adopting a tactical approach brings levity and balance to situations because you remain focused on the issue at hand, instead of getting distracted or veering off in another direction.

_____

_____

_____

LESSON 5: Learn to respond, not react

You might not be able to control the trigger, but you do have a measure of control over the way you behave. If you choose to react, your emotions are in control. By responding, you make the decision to stay in control.

_____

_____

_____

LESSON 6: Build decisiveness

Maintaining an alert state of awareness lets you have enough facts to act decisively when the time comes.

_____

_____

_____

LESSON 7: The Five Maxims of Treating People with Dignity by Showing Them Respect:

1. Listen with all your senses
2. Ask, don't tell others to do something
3. Explain why they are being asked
4. Offer than options rather than threats
5. Give them a second chance

_____

_____

_____

LESSON 8: Display Showtime

Recall the physical and emotional strategies for engaging your professional face when you're heading into a situation, especially one that has the potential for conflict.

_____

_____

_____

LESSON 9: Priming strategies

You can configure your brain to achieve greater personal power when you mentally and physically recognizing the transition into Showtime.

_____

_____

_____

LESSON 10: The Universal Greeting

Launch a successful initial interaction by scripting a response that provides information and lets you get to your point quickly.

_____

_____

_____

LESSON 11: Customize your own Universal Greeting

But knowing what you're going to say and then saying it well exudes confidence, and it can be customized to every situation.

_____

_____

_____

LESSON 12: Listen and build empathy

Understand the other person well enough to find a way to make their wants match up with your objectives.

_____

_____

_____

LESSON 13: Respond with empathy

Empathy is the ability to recognize the feelings and emotional state of others. When you project empathy you increase the odds that others will respond to you favorably.

_____

_____

_____

LESSON 14: Master the art of clarification

When people are in the midst of stress or conflict, they don't always say what they mean. Respond, don't react, to those words and seek to find the meaning.

_____

_____

_____

LESSON 15: How to paraphrase

Listening to another's message and paraphrasing their words back to them lets the other person hear their message played back to them. They'll confirm if you have the message right or not.

_____

_____

_____

LESSON 16: Summarize and move ahead

Once you're clear on the message, you comprehend the situation and move toward resolution. The final stage of the listening process is to recap what you both know, and verbalize where you're going.

_____

_____

_____

_____

LESSON 17: Understand resistance

You need to recognize the difference between legitimate questions and active resistance, and then respond with the appropriate level of persuasion.

_____

_____

_____

LESSON 18: How to handle an insult

Deflect the verbal assault, then redirect them back to your goal by using professional language. But make sure you are listening, because they may have legitimate concerns.

_____

_____

_____

LESSON 19: The Persuasion Sequence

The Persuasion Sequence kicks in when you need someone to modify their behavior. It's a scripted approach to get someone else to stop doing wrong and start doing right.

_____

_____

_____

LESSON 20: Identify When Words Alone Fail

You've tried the Persuasion Sequence and it didn't work. You need to recognize the signs that require you to take immediate action.

_____

_____

_____

LESSON 21: Recognize and address gateway behaviors

A gateway behavior foreshadows worse acts of disrespect to come. When a gateway behavior is ignored it is implicitly being tolerated. By eliminating gateway behaviors, you are setting up a social contract for acceptable conduct.

_____

_____

_____

LESSON 22: Apply these lessons at home

The sign of a robust social contract is an environment in which everyone buys into and helps enforce the rules.

_____

_____

_____

LESSON 23: Observe and evaluate

Bystanders must also interpret the situation as a problem and assess the risks; otherwise, they will see no need to intervene.

_____

_____

_____

LESSON 24: Intervene appropriately

Bystanders are more likely to step into a situation when they understand that low-level intervention options minimize risk and are highly effective.

_____

_____

_____

Children can benefit from verbal tactics, too

As special thanks for reading the book, I would like to offer a free copy of our workbook, Verbal Defense for Kids: a Guide for Parents and Teachers.

To get your free copy of this great resource, visit
www.ConfidenceinConflict.com/Kids

Coming soon ...
more Confidence in Conflict for YOU

Now that you have an understanding of what Confidence in Conflict means in your personal life, you can take these skills to work with this new series of books:

Confidence in Conflict ...
- from the Experts
- for the Health Care Professional
- for the Public Safety Professional
- for the Workplace
- on Campus
- for the Youth Educator

Members of Vistelar's team of consultants hail from a variety of professions. By synthesizing our conflict management strategies with what really happens on the job, they'll take your level of understanding to a whole new level.

For release dates and more information on the Confidence in Conflict book series, visit www.ConfidenceinConflict.com.

Note: While you're on the site, be sure to sign up for the weekly newsletter. It's filled with free lessons and updates for Confidence in Conflict.

"I've discovered we all have the power to become better."
—Bob "Coach" Lindsey,
Vistelar Advisor and 2013 Law Enforcement Educators & Trainers
Association (ILEETA) Trainer of the Year,
as quoted in Confidence in Conflict for Everyday Life

Learning opportunities with the Vistelar Group

- Speaking
- In-Person Training
- Online Learning

The Vistelar Group is a global consulting and training organization focused on addressing the spectrum of human conflict—from interpersonal discord, verbal abuse and bullying—to crisis communications, assault and physical violence.

Vistelar Group clients include all organizations where human conflict has a high prevalence, within business, health care, education, public safety and government.

Our primary purpose is to keep people safe by teaching them how to prevent conflict from occurring, verbally de-escalate conflict if it occurs and physically defend themselves if attacked.

The Vistelar Group provides its training via a national network of consultants and speakers, training partners in specific market segments and digital training programs (online courses, DVDs, webinars) using Performance-Driven Instruction™, a unique approach to training that emphasizes student interaction, real-world simulations, skill practice, memorable stories and physical activity.

Learn more at Vistelar.com

Beyond Conflict: The event for anyone who deals with conflict

For successful interactions in our many facets of life, we can improve at managing conflict with our family, friends, students, co-workers, customers, patients and others with whom we interact.

That's the goal of the annual Vistelar conference, Beyond Conflict. This conference is not about theory. Instead, it will focus on HOW TO deal with conflict, such as:

- HOW TO communicate effectively in the midst of stress.
- HOW TO develop your personal power and become bully-proof.
- HOW TO intervene as a bystander in a safe, but effective, manner.
- HOW TO prevent retaliation by treating others with dignity.
- HOW TO keep safe physically and defend yourself, if attacked.

Learn more at www.Vistelar.com/BeyondConflict

"As a teacher, this is career-changing information."

- Damien Marino
Deputy, Jefferson County Sheriff's Department
Franklin Park, Illinois

ORDER FORM

These training products are designed for personal use and for use within a workplace or organization.
Standard shipping and handling rates apply.

Name of Product	Price	Quantity
Laminated Business-Sized Card: Communicating Under Pressure Chart	$2.00	
24" X 36" Communicating Under Pressure Poster	$35.00	
Additional Books *Contact us for bulk pricing*	$12.00	
Online Companion Course Enhance your learning and build your Confidence In Conflict through instructional videos and real-life examples	$69.00	

ORDER FORM

SHIPPING INFORMATION

Name:_____

Address:_____

City_____/ State_____ / Zip:_____

Phone Number:_____

Email:_____

BILLING INFORMATION (Same as shipping _____)

Name:_____

Address:_____

City_____ / State_____ / Zip:_____

Phone Number:_____

Email:_____

Payment method: Please send invoice _____ Credit card _____

CREDIT CARD INFORMATION:

Credit Card Number:_____

Expiration: _____ / _____

Card Type:_____

Security Code:_____

Signature:_____

Please submit this form to:

Vistelar Group

1845 N. Farwell Ave., Suite 210 | Milwaukee, Wis., 53202

Phone: (877) 690-8230 | Fax: (866) 406-2374 | Email: info@Vistelar.com

To place an order directly online, visit

www.ConfidenceInConflict.com/buy-now

Made in the USA
San Bernardino, CA
27 August 2014